ISBN 978-1-332-21028-2
PIBN 10298700

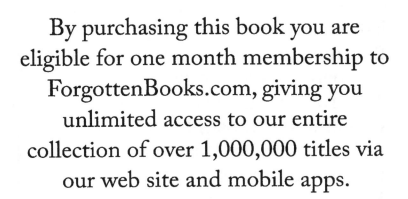

A

WALK

THROUGH

SOUTHAMPTON.

———➤➤◆◄◄———

By Sir Henry C. ENGLEFIELD, Bart.

F. R. S. AND F. A. S.

———➤➤◆◄◄———

SECOND EDITION,

CONSIDERABLY AUGMENTED:

TO WHICH IS ADDED,

SOME ACCOUNT

OF THE

ROMAN STATION, CLAUSENTUM.

———➤◆◄———

Southampton,

PRINTED AND SOLD BY BAKER AND FLETCHER:

SOLD ALSO IN LONDON BY J. STOCKDALE, PICCADILLY,

AND BY T. OSTELL, AVE-MARIA-LANE.

MDCCCV.

IT was at firſt intended in the following pages, merely to give an account of ſeveral curious remains of antiquity exiſting in the town of Southampton, and which had either been totally unnoticed, or very ſlightly mentioned, in the deſcriptions of that place, hitherto publiſhed; and the title of *A Walk* was choſen as expreſſive of what was intended to be done in the work. In compliance with the wiſhes of ſome who ſaw the manuſcript, and to whoſe obſervations and communications no ſmall portion of whatever merit it may poſſeſs, is due,—I have ſtepped beyond the ſtrict limits of deſcription, and have ventured to enter a little into the wide and doubtful field of antiquarian reſearch: but I ſtill hope that my readers will bear in mind the title of the book, and not for a moment ſuppoſe that I aſpire at

the town, and thofe of the bifhoprick, the curious and copious information which they certainly contain.

To the Mayor and Corporation of the Town my beft thanks are due, for the liberal manner in which they permitted me to infpect their regalia and archives; and I fhould do violence to my own feelings, if I paffed unnoticed the affiftance which I have received from an anonymous correfpondent, whofe fingular modefty has not perhaps totally concealed him from my knowledge, and to whofe accurate pen the inveftigators of the beautiful environs of the town of Southampton are, I fufpect, already obliged for one of the beft digefted and moft inftructive of thofe ufeful tracts commonly known under the name of Guides.

H. C. ENGLEFIELD.

DEC. 1, 1801.

ADVERTISEMENT

TO THE

SECOND EDITION.

————«‹◊›»————

THE firſt edition of this work having been
exhauſted within little more than three years
from its publication, I cannot better teſtify
the ſenſe I entertain of a favour ſo unex-
pected, than by endeavouring to render the ſe-
cond impreſſion in ſome degree more worthy
of the public attention. The few changes
which have taken place in the town are noticed; and I thought it better to mention them
in the form of notes, than to alter the original
account. A more extenſive deſcription of the
curious edifice in Porters'-lane is added, from

the account of it prefented to the Society of Antiquaries; and I have given fome etchings of its principal parts. The account of remains of antiquity difcovered at Bittern, in confequence of the building the bridge and forming the road there, is reprinted from my `paper inferted in the fecond volume of the Hampfhire Repofitory, with fome additions. It is hoped that this fecond edition may meet the fame favour which was experienced by the firft.

H. C. ENGLEFIELD.

OCT. 1, 1805.

CONTENTS.

WOOD CUTS.

A
WALK
SOUTHAMPTON.

BEFORE we enter on a defcription of the beautiful and ancient town of South-ampton, it may not be improper to fay a few words on the derivation of its name, on which antiquarians are by no means agreed: fome having fuppofed that it took its origin from the river An or Anton, near whofe fouth-ern extremity it ftands; while others have merely deduced it from the word Ham (a home or place of refidence), which fo often enters into the compofition of the names of our towns, fometimes with and fometimes without the adjunct of Ton. Ham in Surry, and Hampton in Middlesex and Herefordshire, Northampton, and near it Southam, are sufficient examples of this mode of composition; and it is rather curious that the two last quoted names should in this place be exactly inverted in Southampton and Northam. How long Northam has borne its present name, I have no means of investigating; but it seems ·evident that it can only have received it from its situation with respect to Southampton. Yet probable as this really appears, I cannot help inclining to the sentiment of those who derive its more honourable appellation from the beautiful stream which ornaments the central parts of the county, and indisputably gives its name not only to numerous places in its course, but to the county itself. The town of Andover, the village of Abbot's-An, the farm of Northanton and hamlet of Southanton, both near Overton, and not far from the eastern source of the river *Anton*, or rather *Ant*, are abundant proofs of the probability of this etymology: and it may be said, that, by a very natural confusion of two words so similar (particularly in composition) as An and Ham, Northam, from its position with respect to

Southampton, may eafily have received its name, under the idea that Southampton was formed from Ham, not An.

Whether the Antona of Tacitus was the Southampton water, has been the fubject of controverfy into which it is unneceffary here to enter; it is enough for our prefent purpofe, that the Roman Claufentum is evidently formed from the An or Ant, which I conceive to have been the Britifh name of this river and eftuary. To this, the Romans, as was their ufual practice, added the Latin termination, and the Roman name of the river became the Eutum or Antum; and poffibly, by an eafy change, the Antona.

When in the Saxon times Southampton became a place of confequence, the Ant again gave name to the new town, with the Saxon addition of *tun* or *ton*, and we accordingly find Antun or Hantun to have been the early name of the place; as *Wilton*, in the next county, was formed from the river Will or Willy: and this I conceive to be much more confonant to the Saxon mode of formation of names, than the fuppofition that the *town* was called *Anton* from the *river Anton*, without any adjunct, of which, I believe, there is fcarce an example.

But although the confequence of Claufentum evidently declined as the new Hantun
increafed, yet it was by no means deferted;
for there are large remains yet exifting of a
magnificent Saxon or Norman fortrefs or caftellated manfion, built on the ancient Roman
wall of Bittern: and as the new town is fituated directly fouth of the old one, it was natural that it fhould be diftinguifhed from it by
the prefix of *South*. Thus it appears to me
that the name of Southampton was gradually
formed: but thefe ideas are given (as moft
etymologies muft be) rather as matters of conjecture than certainty. By a fort of retro-
grade corruption not uncommon, the river
came, from the town feated on its bank, to be
called in later times the Hampton River; and
the county itfelf Hantunfcyre, as well as its
more proper appellation of Hantefcyre; and
afterwards, by a moft prepofterous confufion
(probably fuggefted by the fimilarity of the
name to Northamptonfhire), the County was
called the County of Southampton. When
this laft corruption was introduced, I cannot
decide; but it is very ancient.

Too much has been perhaps already faid
on this fubject, for a book which pretends to

no deep refearch; too little certainly for a formal differtation on the ancient hiftory of the place: to more laborious inquirers the etymology of *Bittern* and the hiftory of the fucceffive changes of that very ancient place are left: and it is probable that the records of the fee of Winchefter may furnifh much curious matter on this fubject, as Bittern has ever been, and ftill remains, a capital manor and feat of courts holden by the officers of that bifhoprick.

The town of Southampton is fituated on the extreme point of the high gravelly bank which feparates the courfe of the Itchen river from the eftuary of the Teft, or Anton Water. By this happy choice, the whole town, though almoft furrounded with water, enjoys the advantage of the drieft fituation; and the fall of level, in every direction, keeps the ftreets conftantly free from damp and filth. Befides thefe effential benefits, a great proportion of the houfes enjoys a view more or lefs extenfive of the beautiful country adjacent; and as the gravelly foil lies on a bed of clay, numerous wells afford a copious fupply of water fit for moſt domeſtic purpoſes, if not always excellent for drinking.*

As, however, the principal object of this eſſay is to point out the objects of antiquity, or other remarkable buildings, which may attract the notice of a ſtranger, enough has been ſaid on the general ſituation of the town; and we ſhall now proceed to a ſurvey, firſt of the walls and gates, and ſecondly of the ſtreets, together with the churches and other buildings obſervable in them.

The principal and indeed only approach to the town from the land, is by an extenſive and well-built ſuburb; in which nothing occurs worthy of remark,† excepting a large

---

* A very fine and copious spring, which was protected by a large building bearing considerable marks of antiquity, till lately existed in the meadow to the north of the town: it bore the name of Houndwell. The tunnel cut about two hundred yards to the north of the spring for the new Canal, has intercepted the vein which supplied it, and it now is very nearly dry.

† It may not be improper here to mention, that the Canal which is cut from Redbridge to Southampton, and which passes close along the shore of the river, quits the beach about half a mile above the town, and is carried in ·

Elm tree, on the left fide of the road, which is ftill called the Pound Elm, from the ancient pound of the town, which once occupied that fpot. This fuburb was feparated from the town by a very broad and deep ditch; which has been filled up within the memory of feveral perfons yet living. In the plan of the town annexed to Speed's map of the Ifle of Wight, the northern and north-eaftern part of the ditch appears to have been double, having a low bank between the two foffes. On this bank, to the eaft of the Bar-gate, Butts are marked for the purpofe of exercifing the youth in archery. This ditch feems to have been originally cut fo deep as to admit the fea at high water, and thereby completely infulate the town. Hanover Buildings to the eaft, and Orchard-ftreet to the weft, of the Bar-gate,

---

a subterraneous trunk under this suburb. It emerges to the day in the Houndwell meadow, and branches north and south. The northern branch meets the Itchen at Northam: the southern fills the ditch of the eastern wall of the town, and passing under a large arch cut for it through the bottom of the Gaol Tower, opens into the Southampton River immediately beyond it. This work, after a vast expense, has long remained in an imperfect state.

occupy the fite of the ditch; which **was** croffed by an arched bridge leading to the large and extremely beautiful gate called emphatically the Bar. This, it may be obferved, was anciently the name of thofe edifices now called Gates; while the word *Gate* fignified the ftreet or road leading to the *Bar*. At York this ancient phrafeology prevails to this day: Micklegate leads to Mickle-gate Bar, Walm-gate to Walm-gate Bar, and fo of the reft. To return to the Bar: Its north front is of rather uncommon form, being a fort of femi-octagon, flanked with two·lower femi-circular turrets, and crowned with large and handfome open machicollations. The arch of entrance is highly pointed, and adorned with a profufion of mouldings, which now end abruptly; a part of the flanks of the arch having been cut away to enlarge the carriage way, which was inconveniently narrow.

Above the arch is a row of elegant funk pannels, alternately fquare and oblong. In each of the fquares is a fhield in relief, painted with a coat of arms. The bearings on thefe fhields are as follow, beginning from the left:

1. Argent, a crofs, gules. England.
2. Sable, three fwords in pile. Paulet.

3. Argent, a chevron, gules, between three griffins' head erafed, or. Lethieullier or Tylney.

4. Or, two chevronels argent, between three fhamrocks or trefoils, azure or vert. Abdy or Lewis.

5. Argent, fretty, azure, a canton ermine. Noel.

6. Azure, a chevron or between three owls or. Hewit.

7. Gules bordured and croffed or, engrailed : four martlets. Unknown.

8. Parted per feffe, argent and fable, a pale counterchanged and three bears faliant fable, two and one counterchanged, muzzled and chained, or. Mill.

9. Azure, a crofs faltire, argent. Scotland.

And on two fhields below, in the fpandrils of the arch :

10. Azure, a chevron or, between three leopards' heads erafed or. Wyndham.

11. Or, a chevron gules, chárged with three pellets or. Unknown.

Thefe arms are not, however, of an ancient date; as the coat of Mill has the baronets' hand on it, and the creation of that family was in 1619. The arms of Scotland alfo prove

B

that thefe ornaments were added to the gate
after the acceffion of James I.*

The footways on each fide are modern per-
forations through the old flanking towers, and
the brickwork entirely covers the ancient
walls ; but by infpecting the fides of the principal arch, it feems as if there had formerly
been arches opening laterally into thefe towers : if fo, the fcenery muft have been fingu-

---

* On the fronts of the two great buttresses which
flank the arch of entrance, are placed paintings at full
length, and larger than the life, of two warriors, one of
whom bears the name of Bevis, the other of Ascupart.
Although these figures, when compared with the gate, are
modern, yet as they have certainly held their present
places during one hundred and twenty-five years, and are
in a poem of that antiquity spoken of as at that time by
no means novelties, it might seem an omission not to mention them. The connexion between Bevis and Southampton seems of a very ancient date. Whether the old
metrical Romance of Sir Bevis was founded on any fact, I
am not prepared to say ; but the occurrence of the name
of Bevis on the admiralty seal hereafter more particularly
described, proves that the knight was in no small estima-
tion in the town at an early date. It is probable that the
figures on the Bar-gate were placed there at the time that
the arms just described were painted on the ancient
shields. The style of the paintings fully proves that they
could not have been of a date much anterior to James I.

larly magnificent. The arches and front hitherto defcribed, are (though probably four
hundred and fifty years old) modern, when
compared with the central part of the gate;
which is of early Norman work, if not more
ancient than the Conqueft. Its plain' and
maffive round arches, which are confiderably
wider than the outer pointed one, are a full
proof of this. Within this moft ancient part,
another addition has been made towards the
town, forming a plain and flat front; which,
though never very handfome, was much injured in the beginning of the century, by a
moft awkward attempt to adorn it. The
points of its ancient windows are obliterated, a
painted ruftic covers the old wall, and queen
Anne, in long embroidered ftays, and a gown
whofe folds would difgrace even the barbarity
of Saxon fculpture, exhibits her jolly fat face
from a Gothic niche in the centre. The battlements have however efcaped the ravage of
improvement, and an ancient alarm bell hangs
in a niche formed for it, between two of them.*

---

* A very fingular fculptured ftone is inferted into the
wall of this front, juft above the ground, and clofe to the
right-hand jamb of the centre arch. It appears to have

Over the arches is a fpacious town-hall, fifty-two feet long and twenty-one feet wide, to which we afcend by a commodious ftone ftaircafe. Towards the top of this, a large pointed arch is vifible. The hall is lighted by the four windows to the ftreet, which within-fide retain their ancient form, and are rather handfome. At the bottom of the hall, ano-ther pointed arch appears, which opens into a fmall lumber room : the face of the arch in this room is very handfome. The court of juftice is not older than queen Elizabeth's time. A room for the grand jury communi-

---

been the exercise of some apprentice carver, in the early part of the twelfth century, and is covered with faces cut in a very rude style, of different sizes, to the number of eighteen, great and small. One of these is a man's face with a forked beard; another, a female, with a square coif hanging down on each side. These faces much re-semble those which so commonly support the labels of arches, and are sometimes, though more rarely, found under brackets, in the sort of cornices which run round the exterior of the Norman and earliest pointed arched churches. The length of the stone is fifteen inches, and its height is nine inches. As it stands upside down in the wall, and is much corroded, it may easily, though in so conspicuous a situation, escape notice, as it did mine until after the first edition of this book was printed.

cates with the hall, and is lighted by windows towards the fuburb. The grand-jury room is entirely modernifed, but a fmall and dark room adjoining has in it a very curious round arch, with ornamental fmaller fegments of circles within it, and a fmall column on each jamb, in the ftyle of the early Gothic.

The leads are fpacious, and from them the gradual increafe of this noble gate is eafily traced. The original gate is flanked by two femicircular towers towards the country: between thefe, and projecting beyond them, the prefent beautiful exterior front was added: the front towards the town appears the moft modern of all. The two lions fejant, * caft in lead, which now form a refpectable guard to the entrance of the gate, were formerly placed at the extremities of the parapet of the bridge which croffed the ditch, and were removed to their prefent fituation when the ditch was filled up and the bridge demolifhed.

From the gate the wall runs eaftward about

---

* These lions were given (in the room of two others which were decayed) in the year 1744, by William Lee, Esq, son of Lord Chief Justice Lee, on his being made a burgess.

two hundred yards, and is ſtill viſible, though much encumbered with dwelling-houſes; among which, two ſemi-circular towers are barely diſcernible. It terminates in this direction by a high round tower, which has a more modern appearance than any other part of the walls, and ſeems to have been built with embraſures, like Calſhot caſtle, for the reception of cannon. From this tower the wall runs quite ſtraight, and in a direction nearly ſouth, till it reaches the water. At a diſtance of about one hundred yards from the north-eaſt angle, Eaſt-gate formerly flood: it was demoliſhed about thirty years ago, but a drawing of it is among Groſe's Antiquities, and it appears to have been equally ugly and inconvenient. The whole length of this ſide is about eight hundred yards, and it is defended by a broad and deep ditch (in the bottom of which the new canal is dug), and fortified by eight turrets; ſix of them of a ſemicircular form, and two ſquare ones, which, however, appear rather more modern than the others. Theſe two were probably built about the time of Edward VI; as that young monarch, in the very curious account he gives his friend Fitzpatric, of his ſummer excurſion into this

county, fays that the townfmen had fpent
much money in repairing their walls for his
reception. Leland mentions only fix towers
in this eaftern wall, probably the fix round
ones. The upper part of the north-eaftern
tower was probably built at the fame time;
and by Grofe's plate of the Eaft-gate, it had
embrafures fimilar to thofe of this tower, and
moft likely added in the fame repair. The
ftructure both of the wall: and towers is of
coarfe and irregular mafonry: the upper part
is totally deftroyed, and no mode either of defence or annoyance appears, except a very
long and narrow loop, with a circular enlarge-
ment in the middle, near the foot of each of
the towers. Where the wall reaches the fea,
it is terminated by a ftrong tower with a gate.
The arch of entrance is pointed, and has within it two others, of different forms and heights,
and two grooves for portcullifes. Over this
gate is the Bridewell. It feems evident that
originally the ditch was dug fo deep, as to
admit the fea at high water quite up to the
north-eaftern angle of the wall before mentioned; and the projecting tower and building which we fhall next furvey, was very likely
added to defend the fluices, on which fo effen-

tial a requifite to the defence of the town de-
pended, and which of courfe an affailant would
endeavour to deftroy. This mafs of building
is evidently lefs ancient than the walls, and
probably of about the fame date as the outer
part of the Bar-gate. It has been fuppofed
that this tower was built in the time of Henry
VIII, and a paffage in the records of the town
feems to countenance the idea; but it is certainly far more ancient than that prince's
reign; and the paffage in queftion probably
refers to the north-eaftern tower, the more
modern appearance of which has been already
noticed. Its mafonry is much better than that
of the walls, and the windows and battlements
are very neat. It is, however, of a form extremely ill calculated for defence, or rather of-
fence to affailants; and under its fhelter a
large body of troops might advance in fecurity
almoft up to the gate. Its irregular form and
projecting buttreffes render it, however, a
picturefque object. It is now the gaol for
felons and debtors of the town and county of
Southampton.

On the platform juft under it lies a very fine
and curious brafs cannon, of the age of Henry
VIII, and bearing the following infcriptions
and ornaments:

On an efcutcheon crowned with an imperial crown, England and France quarterly;
fupported by a dragon and greyhound.   Under
it, in a tablet,

HENRICVS. VIII
ANGLIE. FRAN
CIE. ET. HIBERN
IE. REX. FIDEI. DE
PENSOR. INVICT
ISSIMVS. F. F.

On another tablet, clofe below the former:

MDXXXXII
HR VIII

Juft before the touch-hole:

ARCANVS. DE. ARCANIS

CESENEN. FECIT

On the breech-ring:

COLOVRINA 4214

Two perforated lions' heads ferve as rings
to lift it.

The ornaments on it are in a good ftyle,
although carelefsly finifhed.

On the fhore, between high and low water
mark, near the platform, ftood the Admiralty
Gallows belonging to the local jurifdiction of
the town.   It is reprefented in Speed's plan of

Southampton, annexed to his map of the Ifle of Wight.

To return to the walls: From the tower and gate juft mentioned, the wall runs in a direction nearly weft for about one hundred and twenty yards, having the fea wafhing its foot, till it meets the Great or Eaft Quay. In this length it is defended by one large and high turret, at which it makes a little bend to the northward. An ancient gate with a low pointed arch, with a groove for a portcullis, and machicollations over it, opens on this quay; which projects into the river about one hundred and thirty yards, and is evidently as ancient (at leaft in part) as the town itfelf. This Water-gate has been fo defaced by houfes built againft it on every fide, that it is not eafy to make out its original form; nor can we now trace out the manner in which it was con-nected with the wall to the fouth-eaft of it, the line of which projects at leaft thirty feet beyond the outer front of the gate. The de-molition of an old houfe built againft it, has lately brought down all the machicollations; and in its prefent mutilated ftate, no one but a ftaunch antiquary could much lament its total removal; which is ferioufly talked of, and which would effentially conduce to the convenience of the commerce' carried on upon the quay.* Juft beyond the northern tower of this gate, two machicollations appear in the wall, which perhaps defended another gate or poftern opening on the quay for the more convenient carrying on the trade of it; but the lower part of the wall is here fo completely blocked up by houfes, that this point cannot be afcertained.

---

* This intended demolition has now taken place, and the whole gate, with the old buildings attached to it, is removed. In apartments above this gate, and immediately adjoining to it, the business of the customs is said to have been anciently transaéted. The two principal rooms were of good proportion, and had wainscot ceilings and ornamented chimney-pieces. Over the chimney-piece of the eastern or innermost room, weie three coats of arms. In demolishing the gate, nothing remarkable was found, except part of a large flat monumental stone, which had been worked into the wall in building the gate. It is of the usual early Norman form, and has the lower part of a figure in long robes outlined on it, and an inscription running round it between two straight lines. The letter of this inscription is of the Norman form, and the words PVR SA ALME PAR CHARITE PRIEZ are legible. A few letters, forming probably the end of the name of the person to whose memory the stone was inscribed, remain, but the name cannot be made out.

From the Water-gate the wall continues in a curved line to the north-weft, with its foot in the fea. Its conftruction is here fimilar to the part already defcribed, and the towers which defend it are much of the fame form, though only partially vifible even from the fea, as wharfs and timber-yards are now built out into the water in front of them. At about two hundred yards from the Water-gate, the wall makes a more fudden bend to the northward, and feems to have fuffered in this part fome injury, either by failure of its foundation, or breach made in it. At prefent it has the appearance of having flipped outwards from the foot, into the fea. At the north end of this part, a high open arch appears in the wall, of the fame fort as thofe which we fhail foon defcribe; and beyond that arch the wall goes on quite plain and very high, till it reaches the Weft-gate. This gate is a low, plain, pointed vault, very ftrongly and carefully defended; there being in its thicknefs at leaft two grooves for portcullifes, and fix fquare apertures for pouring hot water, or other annoyances, on affailants. The tower over this gate is modernifed, but does not feem ever to have been in any way handfome. The length of the wall

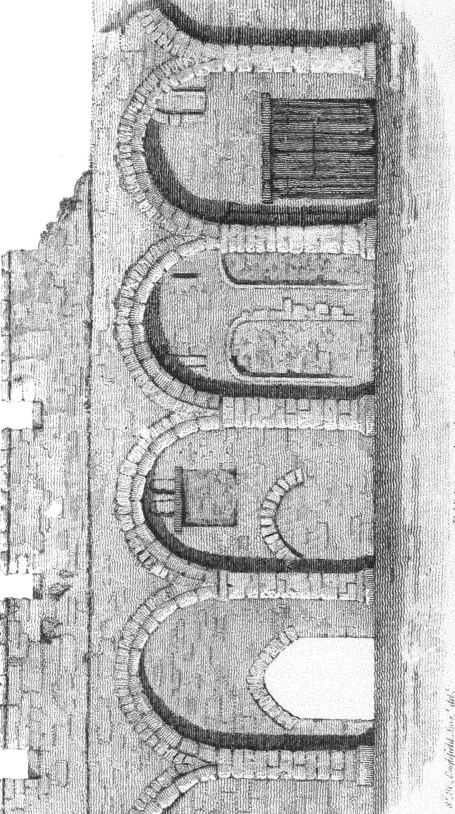

Sr W. Enfield, Bar^t. del^t.

Published as the Act directs Jany 1815.
by T. Baker, Southampton.

from the Water-gate to the Weſt-gate is about three hundred and eighty yards.

The Weſt-quay is ſmall, but, by the caution with which its gate was defended, has evidently been conſidered as of great conſequence, in former ages.

To the north of the Weſt-gate, and fronting the area occupied by the public Baths and Rooms, the wall is of great height, and exhibits a mode of building quite peculiar, and which ſeems ſingularly ill contrived for ſtrength and defence. The wall may here be ſaid to be double. The interior wall has been the front of a row of very ancient buildings; a part of which has been ornamented with Saxon double windows above, and doors of different forms below. Theſe apertures have all been filled up, and againſt the front a row of high and ſlender piers is built, which partly cover the ancient apertures of the wall behind them. Theſe piers are two feet two inches in breadth, and project three feet and three inches from the wall; and they have a baſe projecting four inches and a half every way, which is about eighteen inches high above the preſent level of the ground. At ten feet ſix inches above the baſement, arches are turned from pier to pier;

leaving, however, an open fpace of one foot eight inches, on an average, between the old wall and the new; which are connected by ftones at intervals, leaving interftices fomething in the nature of machicollations, open to the fky. At a confiderable height above the arches, the wall terminates in a parapet, with one battlement in the extent of each arch. The whole range of arches is in number nineteen, but they are not uniform in fize or figure. The firft eight are nearly alike, and are very nearly femicircular; though all, except the two firft, have a flight tendency to a point. Behind the firft, which is twelve feet wide, is the remain of a double Saxon window, with a pillar; and below, the jamb of a door or long window. Behind the fecond, alfo twelve feet wide, appears below, the remainder of the fame door, and another near it with a very flat arched head, like thofe of the lateft Gothic. Above, is a fmall loop to the right, and a double window, fimilar to the one before mentioned, to the left. The third arcade is eleven feet four inches in width, and behind it is a large round arch, of neat plain workmanfhip, and above it a double window. In the fourth, which is eleven feet nine inches in

width, is a very curious small postern, which

into a narrow steep alley called Blue-anchor-
lane. In this lane are to be seen the remains
of two very ancient edifices, of which we shall
say more in the survey of the streets. The
fifth, sixth, seventh, and eighth arches are
each eleven feet wide. The fifth arch has
only a small loop within it : the sixth nothing
but a plain wall. The seventh has a large
modern opening to a court of small houses.
The thickness of the wall may here be dif-
tinctly seen ; and it is very thin for its height

rough pointed arch in the wall. A large pier
then succeeds, with a straight joint all the way
up, against which the arch is turned : this pier
is therefore older than the arcade. A very
flat arch, eighteen feet wide, comes next, with
a thick pier ; and then an arch, six feet four
inches wide, and very flat, with another thick
pier and a straight joint exteriorly. These two
arches and their three piers (together with
another similar narrow arch and its thick piers,
which we shall presently notice) seem as if
they had belonged to a building which pro-
jected beyond the present front of the wall ;

for the face of the fmall arch is rough, as if broken off. This building, whofe ancient form and deftination it is now impoffible even to guefs at, muft have been of great fize and ftrength; and the double walls united at the top by the flat arches, are a very curious and fingular circumftance, and well worthy of notice by thofe who furvey this interefting part of the wall.

The regular feries of arches then goes on. The eleventh, twelfth, thirteenth, and fourteenth, are each eleven feet wide; the fifteenth only nine feet three inches. The eleventh has nothing within it; the twelfth, two pointed door-ways, the one to the right almoft hidden by the pier. The thirteenth has a fmall pointed window or niche, and by it a flat fegment-headed door. The fourteenth has a large femicircular arch, of good mafonry; the fifteenth a flight trace of a window aloft. Then comes in another thick pier with a ftraight joint exteriorly, and a flat arch, fix feet four inches wide, and broken in front like the former. A thick pier with a ftraight joint all the way up exteriorly, forms with this arch a mafs of work very fimilar to the one before defcribed. The range of arches then begins again, The seventeenth and eighteenth are eleven feet wide. The seventeenth has nothing in the wall behind it; the eighteenth has a flat segment-headed door or window, and near it, but lower, a neat large round arch, which extends into the nineteenth arch; which is only five feet three inches in width, and sharp-pointed to range at the top with the rest; and here this very singular construc-

The wall beyond it appears much older, and in it is a low gate with a pointed arch, called Bridle-gate,* over which are the brackets of two machicollations. This gate is merely an arch in the wall, and not, like the other gates, secured by a tower and portcullises in its thickness. To the right hand, just within it, is a pointed arch, which opened into some building now totally destroyed; and on the left, high up, is a door which seems to have opened on a staircase: a narrow arched passage runs through the thickness of the wall over the gate, and terminates at this door. The wall at this gate is five feet three inches in thickness.

D

---

* This gate, in the old records, is called Beidles-Gate.

The wall juft defcribed was certainly peculiarly ill calculated for defence againft any
affailants who could eftablifh themfelves at its
foot, as the demolition of a fingle pier would
inevitably make a wide breach in the arcade
which it ·fupported. It might indeed be con-
jectured, that this part of the wall was wafhed
by the fea (as the parts to the north and fouth
of it ftill are), which would render it lefs eafy
of accefs to fappers or engines of deftruction:
but the regular bafe to the piers,—the Bridle-
gate opening on the area before them,—and
the Blue-anchor poftern nearly at the fame
level, and bearing no appearance of a water
gate,—together with the more ancient numerous ·doors in the wall behind the arches,
which certainly did not open into the water,—
difcountenance this fuppofition ; and the cau-
fes which determined the builders to adopt fo
apparently prepofterous a plan, we fhall probably not eafily divine. The length of the
wall from the Weft-gate to the Bridle-gate is
about one hundred and fifty yards.

From the Bridle-gate the wall makes a fudden projection at right angles to its former
line, of about fixteen yards ; and then, being
at its exterior angle fortified by a fquare tower,

turns back at an obtufe angle : another fquare tower defends this face, which forms a large irregular projecting mafs, beyond the general line of the wall; which then continues in a direction nearly due north, high out of the water, and fortified by fix very ftrong and handfome buttreffes. The third of thefe buttreffes is much larger than the reft, and has in it a door-cafe, high above the foot of the wall, and which probably was a water-gate to the Caftle. In the intervals of the buttreffes are traces of feveral loops and fmall windows, which lighted a large vault; of which more when we treat of the caftle. This part of the wall is beautifully mantled with ivy. The wall then runs northwards in a ftraight and flat face, and has one buttrefs more, at fome diftance from the reft, of moft exquifite mafonry. Juft beyond this buttrefs is a large angular one, which, by flying arches to the wall on each fide, fupported a fmall tower. Here the wall goes off at an obtufe angle to the northeaft, and has three very ftrong buttreffes in this face. At this fpot the wall of the caftle abuts on the town wall; of which more anon. This point is two hundred yards from Bridlegate.

From hence the wall continues of very good
mafonry, ftraight to the north-weft corner of
the town; and it is defended by a very handfome femicircular turret, with a projecting
parapet, fupported by large corbels. The
height of the wall from its foot is here twenty-
eight feet, and of the turret, forty feet. The
tide wafhes the whole of this wall, quite to the
north-weft corner, which is one hundred yards
from the point above mentioned; and the
ground within is almoft level with its top the
whole way; fo that it forms a moft beautiful
terrace to the gardens which belong to the
houfes in the High-ftreet and Caftle-fquare,
and run quite to the wall, commanding an en-
chanting view of the bay, from the town to the
village of Milbrook, and the river beyond it -
quite to Redbridge.

The north-weft angle of the wall is fortified by a very elegant angular buttrefs, with
a projecting parapet fupported by corbels,
forming a fort of fmall watch tower; and very
near it, to the eaftward, is a high and ftrong
circular tower. This angle of the wall has
a very handfome appearance from the water.
From hence the wall runs due eaft to the
Bar, and is about one hundred and feventy

yards in length : one femicircular tower defends it.

ι The total circuit of the walls, as taken from
Mr. Milne's furvey of the town in Faden's
new map of Hampfhire, is two thoufand two
hundred yards, or one mile and a quarter.

HAVING thus viewed every thing worthy notice in the exterior part of the town and its walls, and being returned to the point from whence we fet out on our furvey,—we will now enter the town by the Bar-gate; on paffing which, the moft carelefs obferver muft neceffarily be ftruck with the beauty of the High, anciently called Englifh, Street; which, for breadth, length, and cleanlinefs, can fcarcely be equalled in England. The painter may perhaps lament, that neat brick fronts have in fo many inftances fucceeded to the picturefque timber gables, which not long ago conftituted the principal part of the houfes; but it cannot be denied that comfort has gained what picture may have loft. The gentle bend and gradual defcent of the ftreet, add much to its beauty; as a ftraight level line of near half a mile (which is the length of the High-ftreet from the Bar to the Water-gate) could not but be tirefome to the eye.

The firft object which attracts particular notice, is the new Church of All Saints, built in the pureft ftyle of the Grecian Ionic order, by the late Mr. Reveley; whofe premature deceafe the lovers of the arts will long lament. On entering this church, the bold and graceful curvature of the roof claims high admira-

pews, deſtroys the effect of this building, as it
does of every other ſacred edifice in this country : but a new and peculiar deformity exiſts
in this church, contrary alike to good taſte and
the uniform practice of the church of England.
The pulpit and reading-deſk are placed in the

the altar from almoſt every part of it ; and the
officiating miniſter turns his back directly to
it during the whole of the ſervice. It is to be
lamented, that the Church of England, having formed her liturgy and ritual moſt cloſely
on the model of the primitive church, did not
at the ſame time adopt the form of the ancient ambones or deſks, which ſtood on each
ſide of the nave, of equal height, and from
which in turn the different parts of the ſervice
were read ; inſtead of huddling into one mean
and incongruous group, the clerk's deſk, the
reading deſk, and pulpit, to which the art of
man cannot give either dignity or grace. In
the church which we are now conſidering, the
reading deſk and pulpit might have been
placed, with peculiarly good effect, on each
ſide of the receſs for the altar ; and as the

founding board is omitted, a very elegant form might have been given to them, with no great deviation from the usual shape. As they now stand, besides their very irreverent position with respect to the altar, they have the exact resemblance to the establishment of an auctioneer.

Nearly opposite to All Saints' church is the Castle-lane, and in the wall of one of the corner houses is inserted a stone circular bas relief, with a male and female head facing each other, cut on it. On inquiry I found that this stone was brought with a quantity of others from Netley, in order to be used in the foundation of the house, and was preserved on account of its sculpture. Although much defaced, the carving still appears to have been extremely good for the age in which it was probably done. By the size and shape it seems to have been the keystone of a groined arch; and it is not impossible that the heads on it were those of the founder Henry III. and his queen Eleonora. If so, it is much to be lamented that it is so much injured.

A little lower down, on the east side of the street, in a house lately Harland's Hotel, is a room profusely decorated with very fine carving, of the age of James or Charles I. The chimney-piece in particular, which has the royal arms in very high relief in the centre, and the rofe and thiftle in the lateral compartments, with terms and grotefque figures fupporting them, is executed in a very mafterly ftyle; and the oak, having never fuffered from paint, is of a fine mahogany colour, and as fharp as the day it was finifhed.

The church of St. Lawrence, which is the next objeÉt in the ftreet, is fmall, and almoft choked up with houfes erected round it. The eaft window is not ugly, but the church does not contain a fingle objeÉt either of beauty or antiquity.

Holy Rood Church, which ftands a little lower down on the fame fide of the ftreet, has been much altered on the outfide, but does not feem ever to have been of elegant architeÉture. The weft window is deprived of its tracery, and the tower, which is rather uncommonly fituated at the fouth-weft angle of the church, is void of beauty. The doors of the central entrance are very neatly ornamented with Gothic tracery, in a good ftyle, and well preferved. The colonnade which runs along the

E

whole front, is by the lower clafs of inhabitants known by the name of the "Proclamation." Probably on this fpot, clofe by the old
audit-houfe and market, the magiftrates pro-
claimed peace, war, or other public and official
notifications, which now are promulgated by
the lefs impreffive mode of printed papers affixed to the walls of the principal public
buildings, and often confounded with common
advertifements. In huftings erected within
this portico, the poll is taken at elections of
members for the town.

The church within is large and handfome,
but its appearance is much injured by the organ and its loft, which totally obftruct the
view into the chancel. The nave and fide
ailes are very neatly ceiled in pannels, and the
rofes which ornament the interfections of the
ribs appear neatly carved. At the fouth-weft
door there is a wooden fcreen of mixed
Gothic, of queen Elizabeth or James the Firft's
time, which is uncommonly well executed, and
of elegant defign. In the nave, directly over
and oppofite the pulpit and defk, are two very
fingular long and narrow apertures in the fpandrils of the correfponding arches. The choir

formerly extended to them, and they received the timbers of the rood-loft.

The church had a regular choir, in the manner of a collegiate; a circumſtance unuſual in parochial churches. This ſingularity (which will alſo, be remarked in St. Michael's church) was probably owing to their having belonged to the priory of St. Dionyſius, whoſe monks, on great feſtivals, would perform divine ſervice in them, with conſiderable pomp.*

alſo belonged to St. Dionyſius; having been

---

* It is probable that there was some permanent choral eſtablishment at Southampton; for in the will of the illuſtrious William of Wykeham, a bequest of twenty pounds (a very considerable sum at that period) is made "Domino Johanni Keton præcentori ecclesiæ Suthampton." It is not possible to ascertain, whether the precentorship was attached to any particular church in the town, or whether, by *Ecclesia,* St. Mary's was meant, in opposition to *Capella,* by which we know that the four churches, of St. Michael, Holy Rood, St. Lawrence, and All Saints, were designated, in the charter of Henry the Second. In the same will of William of Wykeham, a vestment and chalice are left, "Ecclesiæ Beatæ Mariæ Suthampton;" and twenty marks, for the repairs of their church, to the prior and convent " Sancti Dyonisii juxta Suthampton.".

all four given to that priory by the fame charter of Henry II. Many of the ftalls yet remain, fome in their places, and fome mixed in the pews. They are of extremely neat workmanfhip and pretty defign, and on fcrolls in different parts of them, the motto of the munificent prelate Fox, bifhop of Winchefter, " Eft Deo Gracia," remains, cut in a very beautiful Gothic letter, in high relief.

The choir or prefent chancel extends beyond the fide ailes, and has handfome windows on each fide, though thofe to the north are now blocked up by houfes. The eaft window is large, but, like the weft window, is deprived of its tracery. A few fhattered fragments of fine painted glafs appear in fome of the windows. Several modern monuments of the Stanleys of Paultons are fixed to the walls of the choir; that to the memory of Mifs Stanley, by Ryfbrack, is the only one worthy notice. In the middle of the chancel ftands a handfome brafs eagle defk. The font, which has been removed from its ancient place near the church door, and now ftands under the organ loft, is octagonal, and adorned with niches, in a neat though plain Gothic ftyle.

The conduit which ftands oppofite the church, is a modern and ugly building. The fprings which fupply it are excellent: they rife in the hill north of the town about a mile, and unite at an ancient ftone conduit-houfe juft under the Polygon, whence the water is brought to the town by a leaden pipe. This conduit is as ancient as the eighteenth year of Edward I, and was made for the ufe of the houfe of Friars Minors, fituated in the foutheaftern part of the town. The water was formerly brought in earthen pipes, formed in lengths of about eighteen inches, and fitting into each other with a fhoulder or flanch. They are ftill not unfrequently dug up in the repairs of the pavement.*

---

* A more copious supply of water is now proposed to be brought to the town, from springs on the highest parts of the common, to the north of the town. The waters of these are to be collected in a reservoir, which will be at so high a level, as to afford an easy supply to every house, as well above as below the Bar. The work is as yet but little advanced; in digging, however, on the common, for the reservoir, several of those bronze instruments, with an edge, and socket for a handle, not unlike large chisels, and which have been usually known by the name of Celts, have been found.

In a houfe nearly oppofite, and now inhabited by Mr. Hawes, is a large room with a very handfome ceiling ftuccoed in compartments, of the date of Elizabeth. A houfe on the left fide of the ftreet, directly oppofite to the Audit-houfe, has a low room on the ground floor with a ftuccoed ceiling in the fame tafte with Mr. Hawes's ; and a large fpace now occupied by a ftaircafe and glafs-ceiled parlour, but which once was a confiderable hall, is decorated with a deep ftuccoed frieze of arabefque foliage, and the arms of queen Elizabeth and her initials, twice repeated. In this houfe, the occupier, Mrs. Cowley, informed me fhe remembered much painted glafs, of which only a fmall fragment now remains.

. The Audit-houfe, which ftands oppofite, on the right fide of the ftreet, is a new and handfome edifice. In it the records, feals, and regalia of the corporation are kept. Of the records I can' fay nothing, except that among them there are feveral charters and books which would repay the labour of the antiquary who fhall infpect them. The feal of the corporation is very ancient and curious. The original obverfe, which is now difufed, and

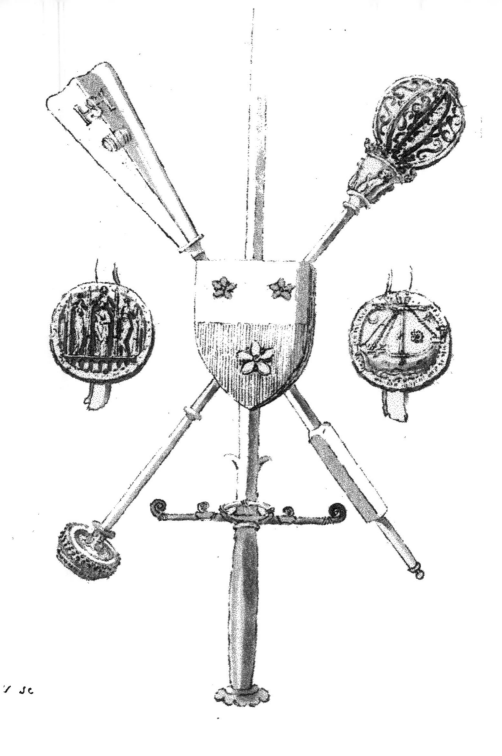

Publish'd as the Act directs Jan.ʳ 1805 by T. Baker Southampton.

nearly- defaced by time and ruft, is of bell metal, about three inches and a quarter in diameter, and bears the impreffion of a single-mafted fhip, on the fea, with the fail furled; and a very high poop and forecaftle. On the deck a figure feems ftanding. Round it, in a fair Roman character, is this legend,—SIGILLUM COMUNE VILLE SUTHAMTONIE. There does not appear ever to have been any armorial bearing whatever on this feal; and the device of a fhip feems to have been common, in early times, to all feaports. The workmanfhip of this face of the feal feems to have been very rude, but the letters are well cut.

The reverfe of the feal is ftill in ufe, and bears a triple Gothic niche, of good defign. In the centre compartment is the Virgin and Child,—in the lateral ones, two figures turned refpectfully towards the Virgin. All the figures are ftanding, and of confiderable elegance in their attitudes and drapery. The infcription round the edge is quite illegible through age.

This face of the feal feems lefs ancient than the obverfe. The obverfe now ufed is of filver, and prefented to the town by private generofity, in the year 1587. Its device is a fhip of war, three-mafted and in full fail, bearing on its mainfail the fhield of arms of the town, party per feffe, argent and gules, charged with three-rofes, two gules in chief and one argent in bafe. This bearing is not probably more ancient than Henry VII, when the hoftile rofes were united.* Round the

---

* Queen Elizabeth, in the seventeenth year of her reign, granted arms to the town of Southampton, which are registered in the Herald's Office, and blazoned as follows:

" Per fesse, silver and gules, three roses counterchanged of the field. The crest and supporters hereafter following, that is to say, upon the helme, on a wreath of silver and gules, on a mount vert, a castell of gold; out of the castell, a quene in her imperial majestie, holding in the right hand the sword of justice; in the left, the balance of equitie, mantelled gules; dobled silver."

" The supporters; out of two ships proper upon the sea, standing in the forepart of the ships, two lions rampant, gold."

In the patent, it is declared, that the town had borne arms long before.

It does not appear that the town ever made use of the cumbrous pomp of crest and supporters, thus added by Elizabeth, to the simple and beautiful coat of arms of the town, and they probably exist only in the Herald's Office, and in a drawing preserved in the Audit-house. The ancient bearing of the arms on the sail of a ship, perhaps,

edge,—SIGILLUM COMMUNE VILLÆ SOUTH-AMTONIÆ. The whole is of bold relief and good work.

There is also a very fair silver seal, exactly two inches in diameter, now used as the admiralty seal. Its bearing is a ship single-masted, and with the sail furled, neatly and boldly cut: on one side of the mast a crescent, on the other a star, and lower down a large rose. The inscription is in a very fine Gothic character, and runs thus,—" Sigillum Majoratus Ville Suthamtone. Beves."

The mention of Bevis is singular, as it does not appear what connexion his name can have with the seal. The form of the letters and style of the work indicate the seal not to be

F

---

suggested the ships as supporters to the lions; and the lions themselves are not unlikely connected with those which now guard the Bar-gate. The crest was no doubt a compliment of the " Queen's Majestie" to herself. For the copy of the grant of arms, as well as many other articles of curious information, I am happy to acknowledge my obligation to Arthur Hammond, esq, of the town of Southampton; whose attention has been long and successfully engaged by the history and antiquities of his native place.

more ancient than the reign of Henry IV.
or V.*

There are six silver maces: two large gilt
modern ones, and four small and ancient.
The most curious of these is probably as old as
Henry VII. It is only sixteen inches in

---

* Three other seals, of brass or bell metal, are kept
among the archives, though now not used. The most
ancient of these is rather more than an inch and three
quarters in diameter. Its bearing is a crowned head, full
faced, with flowing hair, and a very youthful appearance.
The neck to the shoulders is bare, and the robe comes
straight in front, like the old fashion of women's boddice.
On the breast is a castle or tower; and on each side of
the head, a lion passant guardant, as if standing on the
shoulders of the figure: the head of each lion is towards
the face of the figure. The whole is in bold relief, and
not ill cut. Round it, in Saxon capitals, runs the following inscription: S EDWARDI REG ANGLIE P RE-
COGNICONE DEBITORV APVD SVTHT. It has
a ring on the back by way of handle, and on the back is
cut, in a careless manner, but in characters which look
ancient, ADMIRAL.

The " recognitiones debitorum," for the authentication
of which this seal was designed, were evidently those entered into under the statute of Acton-Bumel, of the eleventh
of Edward the First, and usually known by the name of
Statute Merchant. For the security of foreign merchants trading to England, the lands, as well as the chat-

as the Act directs Jan.ʸ 1805 by T Baker & Son Southampton.

length : it has a fmall head with a crown fupported by three fitting lions, and above that,
an open ornament of five femioval leaves, like
the ancient maces of arms : on the top is engraved a rofe, the badge of the town : the
lower end is a large ornamented pommel, with

---

tels of their debtors, were solemnly pledged to them by
deed, sealed with the seal of the debtor, and also with the
king's seal, to be affixed by the mayor or chief wardens
of such town as the king should appoint. The work-
manship of this seal, its perfect preservation, and its
destination, render it a most curious and valuable remain
of antiquity.

A seal nearly similar to this, but apparently of inferior
work, is engraved in Milner's History of Winchester, as
the seal of that city; which, however, it certainly was not
originally; being provided under the statutes de Merca-
toribus, for the express purpose of sealing recognizances,
as its legend shows.

The next in antiquity, is an inch and a quarter in
diameter, and is charged with a leopard's head, full faced,
and open mouthed, with a fleur de lys on each side of it;
above the head are two small roses, and below it two
more. The whole is enclosed in an irregular six-foiled
tracery, of very pretty design, but ill cut. Round the
seal runs the following inscription, in a Gothic character:
Sigillu : officii : stapulle : bille : Suthamptonii : This seal has
an upright handle.

England and France quarterly chafed on it.
The other three ancient maces are made on the
model of this, but not nearly fo old : One of
thefe was not many years fince carried before
the mayorefs, on all occafions when fhe ap-
peared with her hufband in form, as in going
to church, &c ; on which occafions fhe wore a
fcarlet robe or gown.

. This seal is as it were the counterpart of the first.
Edward the Third, following the example of his illustrious
grandfather, in the twenty-seventh year of his reign, extended the advantages and encouragement granted to
merchants by the Statute of Merchants of Edward the
First, by the Statute of Staples. This statute begins by
enacting, that the commerce of wool, leather, and lead,
shall be carried on at certain towns, called Staple Towns,
of which several are not sea-ports, but to each of these
inland staples a port is assigned for entries. It is also
enacted, that in each staple there shall be a seal kept by
the mayor of the staple. Winchester is one of the staple
towns appointed by this act, and Southampton is its port.
The advantages resulting to commerce from the establishment of these offices of staple, it is foreign to this work
to detail. Blackstone and Reeves will furnish ample information.

The alteration of style in the interval of seventy years,
which elapsed between the cutting of these two seals, is
remarkable. The age of the first Edward has very
much the advantage.

The filver oar, the badge of the maritime jurifdiction of the mayor (which is very exten-five, reaching not only over the whole South-ampton water, but half channel over from Hurft caftle to Hayling ifland), is modern, and not handfome. The fword of ftate is very ancient and curious. It is one of the vaft two-handed weapons of our anceftors, with a

---

It may not be improper here to add, that although the jurisdiction of the staple is now totally obsolete, yet the mayor of the town is annually elected mayor of the staple ; and a constable of the staple, and a weigher of wool, are annually appointed, as is enacted in the Statute de Stapullis, chapter 21.

The third seal is nearly an inch and three quarters in diameter, and bears a shield of the form used in Henry the Eighth's time, with a fesse or between three roses, two and one. These were probably the arms of the town at the time when this seal was cut, though different from the arms of Southampton now borne, which in this present form were granted by queen Elizabeth. . On the sides of the shield are a Roman II and a tun, the usual device for Hampton. There is no inscription. On the back of this Seal is cut, ADMIRAL, in the same character, and apparently by the same hand as that before mentioned.

The mayor on all public occasions wears a very handsome gold chain, which, with its medallion, was presented to the corporation by Bercher Baril, esq, senior bailiff in 1792. Previous to that time, no chain was worn.

very fine blade four feet four inches in length, and two inches wide. The guard is of iron (now gilt), one foot and a half long ; and the hilt is likewife one foot and a half, with a large iron pommel. In the council chamber is hung up a good carving of the arms of England in wood, fupported by a dragon and greyhound. Under the coat is a portcullis, and a pomegranate, or fome fruit fimilar to it, and over the crown are two angels hovering. It feems of the age of Henry VII. There is alfo a carving of the arms of Winchefter, quartered with bifhop Fox's pelican, and his motto, " Eft Deo Gracia."

Towards the ftreet there is a very large and handfome room for public meetings.

The ground-floor is open, and, with a large area behind it, forms a neat and commodious market, which is as well fupplied as that of any town in England.

A little lower down, on the fame fide, ftands a very old houfe, the parfonage of Holy Rood church, with a curious ftuccoed front, covered with ornaments. In three fquare tablets appear, in the centre one the feathers of the Prince of Wales, and on each fide a rofe crowned with a clofe crown. The ftyle of thefe ornaments does not allow us to fuppofe them later than the reign of Henry VIII: they are perhaps ftill older. The long duration of this ftucco is curious.

The door of entrance of this houfe, with its hinges and iron ring, is very ancient; and in the fpandrils of the door-cafe are cut, in an ancient Gothic letter, 𝔍𝔢𝔣𝔲𝔰, 𝔐𝔞𝔯𝔦𝔞.

A little lower down, on the left fide of the ftreet, is an old conduit, with a ftone front; and clofe adjoining is, or rather was, the remain of a buttrefs, and fome good Gothic niche-work, which feems to have adorned the conduit, or elfe was a part of the friary, which occupied a large fpace of ground, on a part of which Gloucefter-fquare is now built, and probably in fome meafure with the materials of the old friary.

On another part of its fite is erected a vaft fquare building, which is a very confpicuous object from the lower part of the town. Its original defignation was a fugar refinery, but the project failed; and it has fince been a military hofpital, the fcene of dreadful mortality, from a malignant dyfentery which raged in it; it now is ufed as a warehoufe for the vaft quantities of Spanifh wool, which by *ftrefs* *of weather* are landed here every year.* Human bones are found, in digging for founda-, tions, over the whole fite of the friary.

This religious houfe was founded in the year 1240.

Quite at the bottom of the ftrect on the left, is a large mafs of ftone buildings, now converted into warehoufes, with vaft vaults under them. As there are feveral handfome Gothic doors in this building, it does not feem probable that it was originally deftined for that ufe, to which, however, it has been long applied. This building extends far into Winkle-ftreet, and is feparated from the Watergate by a narrow paffagè, covered overhead by a very old timber houfe, which it is now in contemplation to take down, together with the Water-gate mentioned before. Oppofite to this paffage is a very old conduit, built

---

* England and Spain were at war when this was written, and the commerce for wool was carried on in neutral vessels, mostly Hamburgers or Prussians, who cleared out from Spain for their own ports, but under pretence of damage at sea, put into English harbours, and unloaded their valuable cargoes. The greater part of this trade was carried on at Southampton.

againſt the town wall, with a ſloping roof of hewn ſtone. In the old houſe near this conduit, and now a carpet manufactory, the free-ſchool founded by Edward VI. was originally lodged.

At the end of the warehouſes juſt mentioned, in Winkle-ſtreet, a round arched gateway, with an old turret over it, opens into the court of the Maiſon Dieu, or God's Houſe, founded by two merchants, brothers, in the reign of Henry III. It was by Edward III. given to Queen's College, founded by his conſort Philippa, with which it to this day remains. The chapel is very ancient, but has been ſo defaced by repair, that few traces of its original form are viſible.* An old porch walled up is juſt diſcernible in Winkle-ſtreet. The lodgings of the inmates of the hoſpital

G

---

* In this chapel, the Lords Cambridge and Masham, and Sir Thomas Grey, who were beheaded for a conspiracy against Henry the Fifth, just before he sailed from hence for France, were buried, and a tablet was placed, commemorative of them, by the late earl of Delawar, but there is no ancient memorial of them.

have flat-headed windows of a rather uncommon form.

Returning baek to the Water-gate,—at the
bottom of the High-ftreet, on the right hand,
we enter Porters'-lane; which is fo narrow
and clofed by overhanging old houfes, that it
is difficult to view the front of a very confiderable and moft curious edifice, which has
much the appearance of having been a magnificent dwelling or palace. The extent of its
front to the ftreet is one hundred and eleven
feet, and its height feventeen feet. It is divided into two ftories by a femicircular fafcia
or cord; the lower ftory being ten, and the
upper feven feet high. In the lower or
ground floor, two doors, with flat arches of
fegments of circles, are difcernible; which are
irregularly placed; but the upper ftory is perfectly regular, excepting one fmaller window
at the weft end; and is pierced with a noble
triple window in the centre, with two very
handfome ones, of rather leffer fize, on each
fide. Of the central window only two divi-
fions now remain, but there can be fcarcely a
doubt that it was triple, as otherwife it would
be irregularly placed with refpect to the lateral windows; whereas, under that fuppo-

fition, the whole defign is perfectly uniform.
Thefe central openings probably went down
to the floor, and formed as it were an open
portico in the middle of the room. Their
arch is a very little flatter than a femicircle.
The fide windows had double femicircular-
headed lights, in the ufual ftyle of the Saxon
or Norman windows; but the flat elliptical
arch enclofing them is very fingular. Thefe
windows have a very flat fegment arch within;
and the angles of the opening are finifhed
with a very neat little column, quite in the
ftyle of the early Gothic, with the rib peculiar
to that ftyle, running down the front of each
column. The capitals are neatly carved with
hanging leaves, in the fame early Gothic ftyle.
Thefe pillars and their capitals certainly lead
to a fufpicion, either that this building is not
of fo high antiquity as the exterior front would
warrant our fuppofing it to be, or that they
were additions of a later date than the original
edifice, which is by no means improbable: but
in buildings of this early date, it is not eafy to
fix the period of their erection, with any pre-
cifion. The mouldings of the whole exterior
front are quite in the manner of the early
Saxon, being all imitated from the Roman ar-

chitecture. The impoft of the central window is compofed of an aftragal and cavetto, with a fquare fillet: thofe of the fide windows are a cavetto and fillet: and in both, the fillet is detached from the cavetto by a fingular angular groove or channel, which has a very good effect.

The principal dimenfions are as follow:

Central windows, each, high, feven feet feven inches; wide, from out to out, five feet five inches:

The rife of the arch is two feet fix inches and a half:

The pier between them, wide, two feet two inches:

The lateral windows, high, five feet; and wide, four feet ten inches, from out to out:

The rife of the arch is nineteen inches and a half:

The double lights, one foot fix inches wide; and four feet two inches high:

The pier between them, eight inches wide:

The opening of the window within, high, five feet five inches; and wide, fix feet :— the arch rifes only ten inches:

The fmaller fingle window at the weft end, high, five feet feven inches; and wide, three feet.

The room within does not appear to have been ever divided; but it is fo defaced by modern additions and repairs, that it is fcarcely poffible to fpeak with certainty on the fubject. Its breadth within the walls is fixteen feet eight inches; fo that it appears to have been a fort of gallery. The wall is two feet nine inches thick. In the weftern gable there is a double-headed window, nearly of the fame form with thofe in the front, but of fmaller dimenfions. What remains of the mafonry

of the fmall ftones ufed in general by the Saxon and Norman architects, with courfes of nearly equal thicknefs throughout; a nicety to which the later architects feem fcarcely ever to have attended.

The angles of every part of the buildings are chamfered off, even to the exterior angles of the walls of the front; and in the great central windows the chamfer is rounded, fo as to give the jamb fomething of the appearance of a quarter column. It may be here obferved, that in the infide front of the lateral windows, the arch above the little columns is left fquare; which may confirm the fufpicion that thefe decorations, which certainly are not of the ftyle of the reft of the building, were added at a later time.

No trace, I believe, remains, of the original defignation of this building; but I cannot help fufpecting that it is more ancient than the Conqueft, and perhaps a part of the royal palace inhabited by the Saxon and Danifh fovereigns, who certainly refided occafionally in this town. Its vicinity to the wall, which now chokes up and obftructs its profpect and light, is no objection to this fuppofition, as the wall and Water-gate are much lefs ancient than this edifice.

Immediately adjoining to this very curious building, we come to another of almoft equal antiquity, but in a very fhattered ftate. This building forms the fouth-eaft angle of French-ftreet, which runs parallel with the High or Englifh Street, up to St. Michael's church. The fouth-weft angle of this ftreet is formed by a large and plain ftone building, with a high pointed window over its door, which has much the appearance of a chapel. There is not, I believe, any certain memorial of its original deftination; but it was not improbably the chapel of an hofpital for lepers, dedicated to St. Mary Magdalene, but long before the diffolution annexed to the priory of St. Dionyfius. The arched timber-work of the roof ftill fub-fifts. It is now ufed as a warehoufe.

Proceeding up this ftreet (or northwards), the next object worthy notice is the free-fchool, founded by Edward VI, but many years after removed from Winkle-ftreet to its prefent fite, which was an ancient manfion known by the name of Weft-hall. The dining-room is a very handfome room, with a richly carved Gothic chimney-piece, and a row of windows behind a wooden arcade of a fingular form. The ceiling is of ftucco, in compartments. The whole of this room is at leaft as old as the reign of Henry VIII.

Nearly oppofite to the fchool is the church-yard of the now deftroyed church of St. John, whofe parifh is incorporated with that of St. Lawrence. The area of the church is ftill difcernible, and the churchyard was probably formerly much more extenfive than it now is; reaching quite to the High-ftreet, along Broad-lane; as in digging on the premifes occupied by a cork-cutter, forming the fouth angle of Broad-lane in the High-ftreet, human bones have been difcovered.

A little higher up is the remain of a very ancient building,* which at leaſt three centuries ago has undergone an alteration. This is apparent by the flat-headed arch, inſerted into and partly breaking a very handſome plain ſemicircular one. The ground-floor of this building is a very large cellar now uſed for coals. Nearly oppoſite to this, are very old wooden buildings, called St. John's Hoſpital, in which are ſeveral doors with carvings in the ſpandrils of their flat-arched heads.† Being now arrived at St. Michael's-ſquare, we will return back into Porter's-lane, and by it, enter Bugle-ſtreet,‡ which runs parallel to

---

* This building is called the Weigh-house, where probably merchandiſes were weighed, under the inſpection of the mayor of the staple and the customer of the port; both for the ascertaining the amount of the customs, and preventing frauds or disputes between buyer and seller.

† Since this was written, these buildings are demolished, and their site is at present occupied by a handsome theatre.

‡ Bugle is the ancient name of the bull, and is much in use in this part of England. In Newport town in the Isle of Wight, the principal inn has a bull for its sign, and is called the Bugle Inn. The small hunting horn so much now in use in our army, under the name of the bugle, though at present made of metal, was without doubt, originally, simply a bull's horn.

French-ſtreet, and alſo terminates in St. Michael's-ſquare.

The firſt thing obſervable here is a building whoſe front is in Porter's-lane, and whoſe long flank runs on the right hand (looking northward) up Bugle-ſtreet. This is a ſolid ſtone edifice, with a plain front, much leſs ancient. than the three very ſingular ſemi-cylindrical ſtone buttreſſes in the ſide. Theſe buttreſſes are well built, and appear to be con-ſtructed with a view to uncommon ſtrength. It ſeeems probable that this is one of the an-cient warehouſes of the great merchants of this place, famous of old for its commerce. It may here be obſerved, that in every part of the town there are vaſt ſtone vaults, moſt of them apparently of great antiquity, and con-

H

Perhaps I may be pardoned for here obſerving, that one of the most ancient Welch musical instruments, called the Pib-corn or Pipe-horn, which is formed of a flute, with a mouth-piece not unlike that of the clarionet, inserted into a large horn which forms a trumpet-like termination to it, is still recorded by us in the favourite popular dance called the Hornpipe; and the sweetness of its tones have to this day maintained its use in Italy, under the name of Corno Inglese.

ſtructed when this place poſſeſſed almoſt a monopoly of the French wine trade.

The ground oppoſite to this edifice is only of late years built on, and was known by the name of " the Gravel." When we recollect that this is ſynonymous to The Beach, it ſeems to countenance a ſuſpicion, that this part of the town was open to the ſea until a late period.

Cloſe adjoining to the ſingular building juſt mentioned, there is a long wall, in which are ſeveral doors and windows of different anti-quity, apparently blocked up at different periods of repair. Among them is a ſmall fragment of a very handſome Gothic window. This wall now encloſes the play-ground of the ſchool.

A little higher up on the left, and forming the angle with Weſt-gate-ſtreet, is Bugle hall, of old the ſpacious reſidence of the earls of Southampton, till lately a very fine and ancient houſe, but deſtroyed a few years ſince by fire.

Almoſt oppoſite to it is an old timber and ſtuccoed houſe, with the plume of feathers, the cognizance of the princes of Wales, in its front.*

* In Weſtgate-ſtreet, and very near the gate, on the north ſide, are premiſes ſtill bearing the name of the Linen-hall and Tin-cellar. Tin appears to have been a

St. Michael's-fquare to which we are now again arrived, merits a particular defcription. It was formerly the fifh-market, and was choked up by a building in its centre, where the market was held. It is obfervable, that the fpace between the Caftle and St. Michael's church anciently united thofe fhops moft neceflary to life; Simnel-ftreet, Butcher-row, and the fifh-market: a proof that the town firft grew under the protection of the Caftle.

To return to the fquare. On its weftern fide, and directly fronting the church, is a very large and ancient houfe of timber and ftucco. It confifts of two floors, befides the garrets in its gables. Each ftory overhangs confiderably, and the projections are ornamented with handfome cornices. Little pillars fupporting light femi-arched ribs, run up the front of each

---

very great article of commerce at Southampton, even so late as the reign of Henry VI, who once seized and sold to his own use all the tin lying at Southampton. See Cotton's Posthumous Works. The records of the town also bear evidence of the importance of the tin trade, which was so extensive as to have a separate office for the receipt of the duties payable on it. This office was held (say the records) "at the great house next to Holy Rood church." From the information of A. Hammond, esq.

ſtory, forming the whole into regular compartments. There are four gables of different
breadths, and correſponding to each is a large
window; three of them with curved heads,
and the fourth flat. The lower point of union
of theſe gables has a long and handſome pendent ornament; and very flat arches run from
pendent to pendent, in the ſpandrils of which
broom pods ſeem to be carved, the favourite
badge of the Plantagenets. The gables above
have been moderniſed. At the north end of
this front is a large wooden porch, with a ſingular projection of the next ſtory over the door,
ſupported by a very flat ſemi-arch. In this
porch there is ſome rude carving. The interior of this houſe is moderniſed, but there remains in one of the great windows ſome curious and very old painted glaſs. Many of the
panes have each a bird performing different
offices and functions of human life, as ſoldiers,
handicrafts, muſicians, &c. On the ground-
floor behind the houſe is a large room, now
quite modern, but which tradition ſays was a
chapel. As it ſtands north and ſouth, it was
more probably a great hall. The age of this
very venerable and beautiful edifice can ſcarce-
ly be leſs than four hundred years; and the

wood-work shows high antiquity; as it is, without rottenness, quite perished by age.

On the north side of the square is a mass of wooden houses, now very mean, but in which great marks of antiquity may yet be traced. One door-way with a highly pointed wooden arch is observable; and under a part of these are very capacious vaults.

On the south side of the square nothing occurs worthy notice, excepting a handsome plain semicircular arch, in a building in the narrow alley which runs from the square into French-street, and insulates the church.*

The church itself, which forms the eastern side of the square, is a very curious one, and by much the most ancient of any in the town. The west front has a large window deprived of its tracery. On each side of this, the Saxon masonry of the original front is still discerni-

---

* This arch, together with a smaller arch to the west of it, were probably a part of the wool hall, which extended from them quite to Bugle-street. The low and ancient wooden-fronted houses were erected on its site, and still in the terrar of the town are called by the name of the Woollen-hall. They were all originally one large mansion. For this information I am indebted to A. Hammond, esq.

ble. In the eaftern front the fame mafonry is
alfo vifible, together with a fragment of the
little angular column which occurs fo frequently in Saxon-buildings, and a fmall mor-
fel of a billeted moulding. The length of
the church from eaft to weft, and the breadth
of the nave, are unaltered; but two large fide
ailes have been added, or rather the original
ones have been taken down and enlarged. In
the north aile are two handfome highly pointed windows. The centre eaft window is alfo
very large and handfome, with tracery of rather a late ftyle of Gothic, and fragments of
extremely good painted glafs. The tower,
which rifes from the centre of the church,
is low, and quite plain. A very neat ftone
fpire, of very pleafing proportion and confiderable height, has been added within about fixty
years.

The nave, with its fide ailes, as far as the
tower, is the only part of the church ufed at
prefent for the ordinary divine fervice. It is
feparated from the more eaftern part by an
open fcreen of ancient Gothic, of very good
defign. The old Saxon columns have been,
every other one, taken away; and handfome
pointed arches, of confiderable fpan, turned

the Act directs Jan.ᵉ 1805 by T. Baker Southampton.

over the remaining ones. Their capitals have a fmall fluting on them, of a defign common in that ftyle of architecture.

The tower ftands on four plain and ftrong femicircular arches, without any fort of ornament, except a very fmall impoft moulding. The bells are rung on the ground, and the area of the tower now makes a fingular fort of veftibule to the chancel, which is open to the fide ailes by large arches, and divided from them below by open wooden fcreens. A confiderable number of plain ftalls ftill ftands in the chancel, and many more have been removed, and now ftand in other parts of the church. A handfome brafs eagle defk, which belonged to the ancient choir, alfo remains. The choir probably extended under the tower, as far as the fcreen before mentioned.

In the northern chapel, which is parted from the fide aile by a beautiful open Gothic fcreen, is a handfome monument to the memory of the lord chancellor Wriothefley, and a large and coftly ftanding cheft, carved and inlaid, and ftated by an infcription on its front, to have been given, with the books in it, by John Clungeon. The infcription is as follows:

" John the Sonne of John Clungeon of this towne Alderman

" Erected this preffe and gave certain books who died anno 1646."

The books are however now gone, and the furplices, &c, are kept in the cheft.

In the flank of the north window, oppofite the tomb of Wriothefley, is a fquare funk pannel with a fhield, and a fingular monogram cut in relief in it. A monogram of the fame fort occurs on a ftone on the almfhoufes in St. Mary's churchyard. Thefe are given in the plate of the title, and to them is added another, cut on a very rich Gothic ftone chimney-piece at Romfey. Thefe monograms were evidently the marks of traders and merchants, and occur not unfrequently on the tradefmen's tokens. So much would not have been faid on their fubject, did they not illuftrate a paffage in that moft curious poem called Pierce the Ploughman's Creed, and which Mr. Warton feems to have mifunderftood. (See Hiftory of Englifh Poetry, vol. i. p. 301.)* The

---

* Mr. Warton, in his additions and corrections annexed to the third volume of the History of English Poetry, cor-- rects the mistake here alluded to.

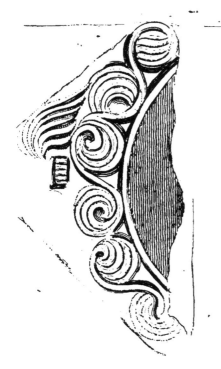

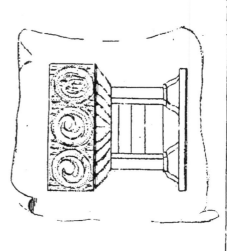

J. Basire. sc.

Published as the Act directs Jan.y 1805
by T. Baker. Southampton.

author defcribing a magnificent church of the friars preachers, fays,

"Wyde wyndowes ywrought ywriten ful thikke
"Shynen with shapen sheldes to shewen aboute,
"With merkes of merchauntes ymedeled betwene."

In this defcription of a window adorned with memorials of benefactors, the "*merkes of merchauntes*" evidently mean monograms of this nature, ufed by thofe who had no right to bear arms, to commemorate their munificence: and as the houfes of the mendicant orders were moftly built by general contribution, thefe marks were very characteriftic of their convents. The abbeys of the feveral orders of monks, founded in general by the devotion of a monarch or fome opulent baron, would for that reafon have few armorial or other bearings in their windows, befide thofe of the founder and his family.

. The fouthern chapel, which has a plain Gothic fcreen in front, and a window to the eaft, of an uncommon though late Gothic form, now contains the font; which is a moft curious and highly ancient one, much refembling that in the cathedral of Winchefter. It

I

confifts of a block of black marble, three feet four inches fquare, and one foot fix inches deep, fupported in its centre by a cylinder of the fame material, ornamented with horizontal rings, fo as much to refemble a barrel; and at each angle by a plain pillar of white ftone, of one foot fix inches high, and about fix inches in diameter. The whole ftands on another marble block, three feet fquare, and about feven inches deep, out of which are cut bafes for the fmall columns, confifting of a flat ring on a large round cufhion. Thefe reft on a plain fquare plinth of about three inches high. A plain leaf falls from the bafes of the columns, on each angle of the plinth.

The top ftone is excavated into a hemifpherical bafon, two feet fix inches in diameter, round which runs a fcroll of foliage, of very rude execution, but not bad defign; and the angles are filled with an imitation of the ancient ornament now generally called the honey-fuckle. A deep groove runs round the edge of the bafon, to receive the cover; and the irons which locked it down yet remain.

In early times the font was fhut with peculiar care, left the confecrated water fhould be profaned, or ftolen for magical purpofes.

The fides of the block, of which three only are now vifible, as the font ftands againft the wall, are each divided into three circular compartments, with a fort of winged monfter in each, fomething like a gryphon ; except one, which has an angel in a long robe of linen, covered with a fhorter tunic. His hands are folded on his heart, and round his head is the nimbus or glory. Behind his fhoulders are two wings, which reach to his feet. Thefe fides are one foot one inch and a half deep ; and the remaining four inches and a half of the thicknefs of the block, flope away to the central cylinder, in a fort of fluting or broad leaves, now much defaced. The workmanfhip of the whole is in the very rudeft ftyle of Saxon fculpture.

It is curious to obferve the effect of time on the black marble of which this font is compofed. A vein lefs hard than the reft runs through one front, and it is quite honeycombed by age, although it probably has always ftood under cover.

Near this chapel is the fouth door of the church ; which has a fcreen before it, with a neat wooden door-cafe, and Gothic capitals cut in the fpandrils. In the wall of the tower oppofite this door, is a low ornamented Gothic arch for a tomb ; but rubbifh is accumulated about it, fo as to hide the tomb-ftone, if there is any.

Oppofite the weft door of St. Michael's church, and clofe by the porch of the large wooden houfe before defcribed, a very narrow and winding alley, called Blue-anchor-lane, leads, with a quick defcent, to the fmall poftern before defcribed in the furvey of the wall. On each hand are ancient Saxon buildings. The late Blue-anchor alehoufe has a good arch in it, and on the left hand we fee the fide wall of that edifice whofe front in the town wall was before defcribed. In this fide wall is a flat-arched door, and above, a double window divided by a column, like thofe in the front ; and near it, a projection of the wall, fupported by plain fquare corbel ftones, which contains the flue of a chimney. The infide of this building is well worth viewing. The accefs to it is by a great modern breach in the front of the arches in the town wall. When within it, we find that there has been a floor dividing it into two ftories ; to the upper one of which, the chimney juft mentioned, belonged. This has a very neat fireplace, of excellent mafonry,

Publish'd as the Act directs Jan.ʳ 1805 by T. Baker Southampton.

adorned with a fmall column on each fide, from which the mantle-piece rofe in a flat arch. The funnel is carried up in a conical form, and the flue is cylindrical. The exterior dimenfions of this edifice, which was very nearly fquare, are as follow :

The front to the fea, fifty-one feet three inches :

Front in Blue-anchor-lane, forty-eight feet nine inches.

Simnel-ftreet, which leads from the Bridle-gate to the upper end of French-ftreet, deferves notice for its name; which is probably derived from the rich cake feafoned high with faffron, a favourite dainty of our anceftors, and not quite out of fashion in Shropfhire; and which was perhaps principally fold in this ftreet.

In an obfcure alehoufe in this ftreet, called the Queen Charlotte, is a room fitted up with handfome wainfcot of the age of Elizabeth; and framed in the wood-work over the chimney is a large upright ftone tablet, on which is cut, in high relief, the following coat :

A chevron bordured between three fhamrocks, two and one. Creft on a clofed helmet in profile, a bunch of fhamrocks :

Motto on a fcroll below the fhield, " Poft
    tenebras fpero lucem :"

Clofe under the fcroll, the initials W. L.

Below this, on the flat of the tablet, " Nullus reprehenfor formidandus eft amatori veritatis. 1579 :"

And on the moulding which runs round the
    whole tablet, "Sculptum Galvie in Hi-
    bernia."

The whole is in perfect prefervation, and by no means ill cut. The letters are very neatly carved in relief, and the D is of uncommon if not fingular form. Thefe arms are borne by a family of the name of Lewis; and the initials feem to countenance a fuppofition, that this coat was placed here by fome of that family. The bearing is alfo that of the Abdy family; but in the repetition of this coat on the out-fide of the Bar-gate, already mentioned, and which probably belonged to the fame family, the colours are different from the bearing of Abdy.

From this ftreet a labyrinth of winding and dirty alleys leads up to the fite of the caftle; which is the only remaining object of curiofity in the town. To defcribe it, we will return into the High-ftreet, and go up Caftle-lane,

merely mentioned before in the ·furvey of ·
High-ftreet. It is moft probable that this
ftreet led to the principal entrance of the Caftle. A fmall fragment of a circular tower is
yet vifible on the left-hand fide of this ftreet,
but built up in a houfe; and the arched gateway was taken down in the memory of many
perfons now alive. The wall of enclofure is
more vifible on the right hand, where it paffes
in a curve line behind fome new houfes, and
continues nearly entire till it meets the town
wall. It is about fix feet thick, and ftands on
the top of a high bank, with a deep ditch at its
foot: This bank has been dug away, fo as to
fhow the manner of the foundation of the
wall, which is on large rough flat pointed
arches. This was probably done both to fave
materials, and to diminifh the danger of cracks
from unequal fettlement. The wall on the
left hand of the gate is nearly deftroyed; it
may however be traced to its junction with the
town wall, near which point a part of the wall
appears in the court of an old cottage, which
has a round-arched window in it, and feems
to have been a handfome building.

Near this fpot, in the narrow ftreet which
leads from the Caftle to Bridle-gate, an arched

gateway was deftroyed about thirty years ago; and in the garden of the old houfe adjoining, there was a vaulted room of very confiderable dimenfions, which received light from the loops and windows mentioned in the furvey of this part of the town wall. This room, by the account of an elderly bricklayer who affifted in its dilapidation, was groined, and adorned with handfome ribs with mouldings, and, as he told me, had much the appearance of a place of worfhip. The ribs and all the convertible ftones were taken away, and the vault clofed up, and fo it at prefent remains.

The area of the Caftle was of a form approaching to a femicircle, or rather a horfe-fhoe, of which the town wall to the fea formed the diameter. The keep ftood on a very high artificial mount in the fouthern part of the area, and probably, as was generally the cafe, in the line of the wall. A fmall modern round tower has been built of the materials of the ancient one, which muft have large, as well as " fair," to ufe the words of Leland.

The high mount and circular form of the keep, indicate an antiquity much higher than the time of Richard II, who probably only repaired and ftrengthened the caftle.* The great beauty of the mafonry in that part of the town wall which formed the enclofure of the caftle towards the fea, and which, it may be obferved, is built of a ftone very different from the reft of the wall, indicates its having been reftored in the reign of this monarch, when architecture had attained a very high perfection in this country.

K

---

* This conjecture is reduced nearly to a certainty by the following extracts, which I owe to the kindness of A. Hammond, esq.

1153. From a compromise between king Stephen and prince Henry, the bishop of Winchester was to give security for the delivery of the castle at Southampton to prince Henry, on the death of Stephen.—Carte.

1246. Commune Villæ Sudhamtoniæ debet cclxx marcas, pro substractione plurium consuetudinum pertinentium ad castram Sudhamtoniæ et de maeremio, plumbo, et lapidibus ejusdem castri prostrati venditis.—Madox.

1340. Richard Talbot, of the Shrewsbury family, was governor of Southampton castle.

1377. In the first year of Richard II, the French attacked Southampton, but were soon repulsed by the earl of Arundel, governor of the town, who assembled the militia. To protect the harbour and town for the future, the king built a castle on an high raised mount.—Smollet.

To this account of the caſtle we have only to add, that a walk to the top of the keep will amply repay the trouble of the aſcent. The beauty of the view is almoſt unrivalled; and the town itſelf, which we have lately been viewing in detail, lies at the feet of the obſerver from this point as in a map, ſhowing, better than from any other ſpot, the whole compaſs of the walls, the courſe of the ſtreets, and the relative poſitions of the moſt remarkable buildings.

It might appear a negligent omiſſion, if the church of St. Mary's, in the ſuburb, was entirely unmentioned; but in truth, although

---

These extraćts leave scarcely a doubt that Southampton castle was one of those which was dismantled in the general destrućtion of fortresses at the end of the reign of king Stephen; and the curious passage from Madox proves that the dilapidations were carried to a great pitch. When, therefore, Richard II. (in order to secure the town from the repeated attacks of the French and others) restored the castle, he had probably such repairs to make, as were nearly equivalent to a new building; and the current tradition, that he was the builder of the castle, is only false, inasmuch as it supposes, that no castle was existing at a more ancient period.

tradition reports it to have been the fite of the original town, yet it at prefent contains no remnant of the antiquity to which it lays claim. The church has been rebuilt within a century on the old foundations, which ftill appear a few feet above the ground; and its fpacious and well peopled church-yard does not contain a fingle object worthy of particular mention. The very large parfonage-houfe has the air of a melancholy manor-houfe of the era of king William, with long fafh-windows and narrow piers.*

From the church-yard, a road not very wide, and bordered on either hand by a deep and muddy ditch, leads to the ancient mill called the Chapel mill. In this road, inconvenient as it is, an annual fair is held on Trinity Monday, Tuefday, and Wednefday. This fair is opened by the mayor and bailiffs, with much ceremony, on the preceding Saturday afternoon. The mayor erects a pole with a large glove fixed to the top of it, near the miller's houfe; and the

---

* In February, 1802, this parsonage-house was entirely destroyed by fire; and a smaller edifice, of very neat architecture, supplies its place.

bailiff then takes poffeffion of the fair, as chief magiftrate in its precinct during the fair, and invites the mayor and his fuite to a collation in his tent. He appoints a guard of halber-diers, who keep the peace by day, and watch the fair by night. During the fair, no perfon can be arrefted for debt within its precincts. On the Wednefday at noon, the mayor dif-folves the fair, by taking down the pole and glove, or rather ordering it to be taken down; which till lately was done by the young men of the town, who fired at it with fingle balls, till it was deftroyed, or they were tired with the fport. Probably it formerly was a mark for the lefs dangerous dexterity of the young archers.

This fair was granted by one of the Henrys, but by which of them is not quite certain, to the town of Southampton, and William Geoffry, hermit of the hermitage of the Holy Trinity and Bleffed Virgin Mary. The fite of this her-mitage is now the Chapel mill, which ftill has marks of antiquity about it; though its en-largement, about fixty years fince, has left but little of its ancient ornaments, except a flank of a door, and part of an arched window. Thefe fragments, however, fhow that the ftyle of its architecture much refembled the chapel of St. Dionyfius at Portfwood. The miller's

bones are ftill dug up there. In digging near it, about thirty years fince, for the purpofe of building the Renown frigate, a fkeleton and a ring were found.*

.From hence the walk to the Itchen ferry, at high water, is very beautiful, commanding a view of the oppofite fteep and woody fhore, and enlivened with a multitude of veffels of different fizes, laid up or under repair. The little round building called the Crofs-houfe, erected for the accommodation of paffengers waiting for the boat, has marks of confiderable antiquity, and is not an ugly edifice. In one of the quarters are the arms of Southampton, with the date only of 1634: but parts of the building feem to be of much earlier date. At this point, the ferrymen of the Itchen ferry do homage to the mayor and corporation, when-

---

* A large and curious silver ring was found about fifty years ago in the field opposite the miller's house. It is in the possession of Arthur Hammond, esq; and has been well engraved in the Gentleman's Magazine for November 1802, but I cannot pretend to explain the inscription on it.

ever the perambulation of the boundaries of the town is performed; and in return for the permiffion of landing on the demefne of the town, engage at all times to carry over gratis the burgeffes and their families.

From this point, a cauffey of near half a mile long, planted with trees, leads to the platform and fouth gate. This walk, which is called the Beach, commands in its whole length a view of the Southampton water, clofed by the Ifle of Wight; and it is not eafy to imagine a more beautiful or interefting water fcene. The view of the town is alfo pretty, and the new church of All Saints appears from hence to great advantage. It is to be lamented, that the marfhy meadow clofe to the cauffey is not drained and improved. The falubrity of the town, and above all of the fuburb of St. Mary's, calls loudly for it; and the ground in an enclofed or even a drier ftate, would amply repay the expenfe; but contefted rights of common have (in this as in a thoufand other inftances) hitherto prevented that being done, which every body feparately approves.

Before I at the Water gate difmifs the reader, who may have had the patience to accompany me through the narrow and dirty paths, and into the holes and corners, to which I have led him, I cannot forbear making an obferva-tion on the peculiar character of the antiquities we have been furveying. Among the many fpecimens of the round-arched mode of build-ing, commonly called Saxon, not a fingle piece of carving exifts, except the fmall columns within the window in the edifice in Porter's-lane, and a few leaves juft fketched on the capitals of the little pillars in the building co-vered by the arches in the wall near Weft-gate; nor an ornamented moulding, except a fmall fragment of billeted fafcia, at the eaft end of St. Michael's church. The carved mem-bers of impofts and arches, fo profufely ufed by the Normans, and particularly their favourite zigzag, do not appear ever to have exifted in any of the buildings now extant in the town; and a great number of the arches, both of the doors and windows, of inconteftably high anti-quity, are flatter than a femicircle; fome being fegments of circles, and fome femi-ellipfes, The mouldings of their impofts and fafcias are alfo in exact imitation of the Roman architec-ture, having very well formed quarter-rounds and cavettos, From thefe confiderations I cannot but be led to fufpect, that they are of an antiquity confiderably greater than the Norman era ; and I hope that thofe antiquaries who may differ from me in opinion, will at leaft acquit me of having taken it up without fome grounds.

I HAD here purpofed to take my leave of thofe readers who have thus far borne me company; as my firft intention was fimply to have noticed and defcribed thofe objeɗs which now exift, worthy the attention of the curious. But having infenfibly been led into feveral ob-fervations which rather pafs the line I had firft laid down, I fhall trefpafs yet farther on the patience of my companion, and fay a few words on the ancient fituation of the town of South-ampton, and its gradual removal from its ori-ginal to its prefent fite. In a difcuffion of this fort, much muft reft on conjeɗure; yet I truft that my ideas will be not unfupported by the teftimony of monuments ftill fubfifting.

That the Romans had an eftablifhment of confiderable confequence on the fpot in the vicinity of this town now known by the name of Bittern, is inconteftably proved by the re-mains of their walls yet exifting, and the nu-merous fragments of antiquity lately brought to light in forming the road to the new bridge; and there feems very little doubt that this was the ancient Claufentum.*   The hamlet of Northam, which ftands directly oppofite to Bittern, on the fouthern bank of the Itchen, was probably in fome degree inhabited at the fame period; as coins are faid to have been found there. It is probable that the mouth of the Itchen was at that time, and long afterwards, much wider than it now is, and that the water flowed in nearly a ftraight line from Northam to St. Mary's churchyard, and from thence to the prefent fouth gate, in a curve, not far from the line of the town wall, covering the whole Marfh, and the fite of the buildings on the fame level now called Orchard-lane, Springgardens, &c.   Nothing, indeed, but artificial embankments, prevents the fea, at high water, from inundating thefe places at the prefent day.

In this line, the diftance from Northam to St. Mary's is not great; and the fprings of Houndwell would naturally draw the inbabitants of Northam from a fpot without water to one fo well fupplied with that moft neceffa-

L

---

* A further account of Bittern is given in the appendix.

ry article, and at leaſt equally well ſituated
for fiſhing, or other nautical occupations.
This probably was the ſtate of things, until the
Saxon conquerors of the kingdom, having
formed permanent eſtabliſhments in the country from which they had nearly ſwept its ancient inhabitants, began to wage perpetual in-
teſtine wars, and of courſe to fortify the moſt
important poſts, after the manner of their own
nation. The eſtabliſhments of the Romans,
which ſeem to have been ſeated in general in
low ſituations, and near ſtreams, did not at all
ſuit with the northern ſyſtem of fortreſſes;
which, particularly in the earlieſt times, affect-
ed elevated ſites, with high towers, ſecured
from ſurpriſe, by the view they commanded of
the country around them; and from aſſault,
by the ſteep aſcent of the natural or artificial
mount on which they were founded. The
peculiar advantages of the narrow and rather
high point of land on which Southampton now
ſtands, commanding at once the Itchen and
Teſt, and very eaſily fortified on the land ſide,
could not eſcape their notice; and from the
high circular hill on which the keep of the
caſtle formerly ſtood, and the curved line of its
yet remaining wall, we have probable grounds

for fuppofing it to be among the moft ancient of the Saxon caftles. But befides the prefent exifting fortifications, there is great reafon to fufpect that the northern ditch of the town, filled up within the memory of man, and of uncommon breadth and depth, was continued quite acrofs, till it met the Itchen, and completely infulated the caftle and prefent town. The antiquity of the Bar-gate, whofe central round arch is evidently much older than any of the other gates of the town, is no fmall confirmation of this fuppofition ; as the walls and gates, with the exception of the Bar-gate, ap-, pear to have been built at once, and are very uniform in their ftructure, fome fmall parts only excepted, which we fhall confider more particularly prefently.

It is, however, immaterial to the view of the progreffive augmentation of the prefent town, whether this conjecture, relative to the Bar-gate and its ditch, be founded or not ; as it is equally certain, under either fuppofition, that the caftle would very foon form a town around itfelf; both by the habitations of thofe who were dependent on it as a fortrefs, and thofe who fought protection under its wings, from the multiplicd dangers of that period of uncea- .

fing war and pillage. The very ancient church of St. Michael was probably founded foon after the caftle, and was, as it now is, the manerial church of the town: and it is worthy of remark, that the ftreets immediately under the caftle, are proved, by their names, to have been the original markets of the infant town; and that all the moft curious remains of antiquity ftretch along the fhore of the Southampton water, where the caftle protected them on the land fide, and the fea rendered attack not very eafy on any other.

The appearance of the very interefting building in Porters'-lane, and the fingular fquare houfe now making part of the wall near Blue-anchor-lane, is that of houfes for the habitation of fecular perfons of confequence; as neither of them, particularly the former, has the leaft appearance of a conventual edifice; and it is not at all improbable, that the Saxon kings might have a palace on the fhore, commanding, as the building in Porters'-lane did, until the town wall was erected, a beautiful view of the fea, with a fouthern expofition, and a fheltered fituation. The hiftory of Canute's rebuke to the impious flattery of his courtiers, and which the moft authentic hiftorians ftate to have

taken place at Southampton, proves that the
town was of confequence in his time; and it
is much more probable that the regal chair
was placed on the fandy fhore of the Southampton river, than in the black and oozy bed
of the Itchen at Northam, where fome have
fixed the fcene of this ftriking and characteriftic ftory.

The very ancient hofpital of God's-houfe,
whofe round-arched gate, and very obtufely
pointed double-headed window over it, place
its erection early in the twelfth century; was
probably built before the exiftence of the
prefent wall, which makes an odd and irregular curve outwards, feemingly with a view
to leave a paffage, though a narrow one,
before the church, which once had a door
and porch projecting into the ftreet.

But independent of all conjecture, there
exifts an indifputable proof of the early confequence of the prefent town of Southampton.
Henry II, in a charter given by Dugdale in
his Monafticon (vol. ii. p. 109), gives to
the priory of St. Dionyfius, the churches of St.
Michael, Holy Rood, St. Lawrence, and All
Saints, in the following words:

"Sciatis me dediffe et conceffiffe Deo et
"Ecclefiæ Sancti Dionyfii juxta Hamtonam,
"&c. Capellas meas quas habebam infra
"Burgum de Hamptona, &c. fcilicet Capellam
"Sancti Michaelis, et Cap. Sanctæ Crucis,
"et Cap. Sancti Laurentii, et Cap. Omnium
"Sanctorum. Quare volo, &c."

This charter fully proves that the four
prefent churches were in exiftence fo early as
the reign of Henry II, nor are they fpoken of
at all as new erections, but as having been
fome time in the gift of the crown; "quas
habebam." It may alfo be remarked, that
they are all called "Capellæ," *Chapels;* St.
Mary's being probably confidered as the "Ec-
"clefia," or *Church,* within whofe parifh they
were erected. St. Michael's is alfo named
firft, as having then, as it now has, the prece-
dence over the reft.

We cannot defire fuller proof, that the town
was then nearly or quite as large as it now is.

With refpect to the date of the building of
the wall as we now fee it, difficulties arife
in my mind. It is certain, that the nor-

and the gates of the town are apparently of the fame date with the walls, and much refemble each other in the maffy flat form of their pointed arches, which rife at an angle from their piers, being ftruck from centres below the level of their fpring; a mode of conftruction ufed about the time of Edward II; yet the remains of femicircular towers ftill vifible on attentive infpection of the Bargate, and which flanked its round arch, very much refembling, in form and mode of building, the towers of the north and eaft wall, lead me to fufpect, that the wall, on the land fide at leaft, is of higher antiquity than the time of the Edwards, and that the prefent gates were built later than the erection of the wall. The very fingular fituation of the Water-gate, which retires thirty feet behind the line of the eaftern part of the fouth wall; and the odd pofition of the fouth gate, at the very angle of the wall; feem to indicate that thefe gates were not of the original defign.

From the fouth-weft angle of the wall quite to the Bridle-gate, which was clofe to the ballium of the caftle, the whole wall is a mafs of irregular and almoft inexplicable conftruction. I cannot help being fufpicious, that this fide of the town, protected as it was by the caftle, and covered by the fea, was not at all, or very flightly, fortified, until the fatal experience of the fack of the town, by the French invaders, had proved that fome further defence was neceffary. This conjecture receives confiderable ftrength from the appellation of " the Gravel," mentioned before to have been given to the lower end of Bugle-ftrect, and which can fcarcely be referred to any other origin, but this part of the town having been long open to the fea, and free from buildings. It may alfo be obferved, that both French and Bugle ftreets now terminate moft awkwardly againft the wall, which comes fo near as to leave only a very narrow lane of communication between them, and feems to have been erected long after thefe ftreets were built and inhabited.

At this part I conceive the invaders to have attacked and entered the town ; and the buildings incorporated in the wall near Weft-gate and Bridle-gate, were perhaps fo far ruined by their fires, as to be deferted by their inhabitants, and relinquifhed by them for the purpofe of fortifying this vulnerable part of the town. Although, at this diftance of time, no great ſtreſs can be laid on the appearance of walls ſo long expoſed to the weather, yet it is certain, that the eaſtern wall of the very ancient edifice forming part of the town wall and flanking Blue-anchor-lane, has very much the appearance of having been reddened by violent fire.

The line of wall ſouth of the Weſt-gate is irregular in its conſtruction; and the wall between Weſt and Bridle gates, which has been already deſcribed, bears evident marks of having been built in the moſt haſty manner, and with the greateſt economy of materials; which ſeems the only way of accounting for the raiſing the parapet on thoſe ſingular arches we now ſee, and the forming the wall of old fronts of edifices full of apertures, which muſt of neceſſity weaken walls even without them not very thick or ſolid. This wall, in its preſent form, I con-ceive to have been built about that period, when the old hiſtorians ſtate Richard II. to have fortified the town, and built the caſtle; which he probably repaired and ſtrengthened, but which evidently had been built ſeveral centuries before his time.

M

Whatever may be the opinion of different perſons, reſpecting the age of the ſeveral parts of the town and its walls already mentioned, one thing is indiſputably certain, that the town was not removed to its preſent ſite, as has been aſſerted by Leland, and after him by Groſe in his Antiquities, in conſequence of the deſtruction of the old town at St. Mary's, by the French or Genoeſe, in the year 1338. Indeed, the roll of parliament quoted by Groſe, ordering the town to be fortified in the very next year, is a full proof of itſelf that the diſaſter happened to the preſent town ; as it would have been impoſſible for the inhabitants, ruined by pillage and fire, in that ſpace of time to have built a large town from the ground, on a new ſite; whereas the repairs of a place which had ſuffered, however ſeverely, from plunder and conflagration, are done with much leſs expenſe, and in a very ſhort period. It is, however, highly probable, that the old town of St. Mary's, never very conſiderable, and which would naturally decline in proportion to the increaſe of the new town, being totally deſtitute of defence, ſuffered yet more ſeverely than Southampton itſelf ; and its deſtruction might be much accelerated by this difafter ; as few would rebuild their houfes without the walls, who could by any means find habitations within them.

From this period to the prefent time, the hiftory of the town as a fortified place, may be comprifed in a few words. Edward VI. fpeaks of repairs done to the walls by the citizens for his reception ; and from his time to the pre-fent day, they have probably never been touched but for their deftruction. The in-creafing ftrength of the nation, and yet more the augmented fize of fhips of war, now too large to enter with fafety thofe rivers and creeks, which formerly were the moft fecure havens, have combined to infure from attack the ancient ports of this country ; and the walls of our cities are, by a felicity on which every Englifhman will reflect with gratitude and refpect, rendered merely ornaments to thofe towns where every houfe is a caftle to its owner, fenced by laws ftronger than the bra-zen walls of Merlin. That this glorious bul-wark may be alfo " ære perennius," is a wifh in which all, I truft, will join, but the anti-quary with peculiar feeling, who views it not merely as a prefent impregnable guard, but as the venerable work of his forefathers.

APPENDIX.

ACCOUNT

OF AN

$\mathcal{A}\mathcal{N}CIE\mathcal{N}T$ BUILDING

IN

SOUTHAMPTON.

—➤➤◆◄◄—

By Sir H. C. ENGLEFIELD, Bart. F. R. S. & V. P. A. S.

—➤➤◆◄◄—

Read before the Society of Antiquaries of London, April 16, 1801.

ACCOUNT

OF AN

ANCIENT BUILDING

In SOUTHAMPTON, &c.

THE building, of which I have now the honour to lay before the Society the meafured drawings, is fituated in the fouthern part of the town of Southampton, in a narrow ftrect called Porters'-lane, not far from the Water-gate at the bottom of the High-ftrect.

That it has hitherto efcaped the notice of the curious, is probably owing to its prefent very confined fituation. The ftrect in which it ftands is barely wide enough to admit a cart, and is generally full of carriages of burthen; and a footpath has been gained out of the ground-floor of warehoufes on the oppofite fide of the way, which forms an open gallery, but fo low, that from it a paffenger can only fee the lower part of the building in queftion; which is fo

N

defaced by modern openings for doors and windows, as to excite in the inattentive paſſer by, no curioſity for a further inſpection. The whole of the building is now converted into ſtables below, and haylofts above; and of ſo difficult and dirty acceſs, that it is not an eaſy matter to take either meaſures or drawings of it.

Although its preſent ſite is ſo confined, at the period of its erection it enjoyed an open and beautiful view of the Southampton river and oppoſite ſhore; as the town wall, which at preſent runs parallel with its front, is evidently of a date very much more modern; and the large windows ſeem calculated for the full enjoyment both of the air and ſouthern ſun, to which it is directly expoſed.

No part of the preſent remains has the appearance either of having been conſtructed for religious purpoſes, or for thoſe of defence; nor is there any trace of a religious eſtabliſhment having at any period exiſted in this part of the town; the building was therefore, probably, conſtructed for a dwelling-houſe, and its ſize and magnificence may juſtly entitle it to the name of a palace.

The front extends one hundred and eleven feet, and, as the angles of the wall are in fome parts perfect at each end, it is certain that this was the original extent of the front of the building. The prefent height from the ground to the top of the wall is feventeen feet. There is reafon to think that the wall never was much, if at all, higher; but it is almoft certain that the bottom of the building is buried at leaft two feet, as the jamb of the ancient flat-arched door is now only four feet fix inches above the pavement, which is much too low for the common purpofes of life. The elevation is, however, from the prefent level of the ftreet.

At ten feet from the ground runs a faſcia, which divides the external front into two ftories. In the lower ftory are the remains of two ancient doors, irregularly placed; of thefe, however, one does not feem coeval with the original building.

Above the fafcia the wall rifes feven feet, and, with the exception of a fmall window at the weft end, it is perfectly regular in its defign, and the diftances and openings of the windows.

Three magnificent windows occupy the centre of the front. Of thefe, two only now remain; but as the defign is totally irregular if a third be not fuppofed, and perfectly regular if it be, and as triple openings were almoft conftantly ufed in our ancient buildings, there can be no doubt that there were originally three windows.

The opening of thefe windows is, in front, feven feet feven inches high, and five feet five inches wide, and the pier, which divides them, is two feet two inches broad; their arched head is very little flatter than a femicircle. A very neat moulding ranges over the arches. The angle of the wall is rounded off, fo as almoft to have the appearance of a quarter column. Ten inches and a half from the front, the wall breaks in, fix inches, and reduces the opening of the real window to four feet four inches wide, and feven feet one inch high.

The bottom of thefe windows is built up, fo that the exact termination of them is not eafily afcertained. They, however, certainly defcend two feet below the general line of the fafcia before mentioned.

The interior face of thefe windows is quite plain, except that the angle, like the exterior ones, is chamfered off.

At nine feet from the exterior angles of thefe windows, are two others, one on each fide. Thefe windows are four feet ten inches wide from out to out, and five feet high; and their bottom refts on the fafcia. They are covered by a very flat elliptical arch, whofe rife is only one foot feven inches and a half. The arch fprings from a plain impoft, and a moulding of the fame defign ranges round each arch. Thefe windows are divided into two lights, as was ufual in the Saxon and Norman buildings. Thefe lights are four feet high, and one foot fix inches wide, in the clear. All the angles of thefe windows are neatly chamfered off. The decoration of the interior of thefe windows is very fingular; a very neat column, with a regular bafe and a capital adorned with leaves, and furmounted with a fhort cornice or impoft, adorns each angle. Thefe columns are excavated as it were out of the angle; and do not project beyond the faces of the wall. The whole air and proportion of thefe columns, are more like that of the early Gothic, than the Norman ftyle; and the little rib which runs down the fhaft is almoft peculiar to the early Gothic. It is alfo obferveable, that the very flat arch which covers the window within, and which only rifes ten inches on an opening of fix feet, is the only part of the building which has not its angle chamfered off. Thefe circumftances lead to a doubt whether this decoration, fo different in ftyle from the reft of the building, may not have been an addition at a period later than the original edifice. If this part is coeval with the reft, the building itfelf muft be efteemed of the age of Henry I. or thereabouts; although, from every other part of it, I fhould have been led to fuppofe it at leaft as old as the Conqueft, if not confiderably more ancient.

At eleven feet from thefe windows, are two others, exactly fimilar, except that the eaftern window has a double impoft, owing probably to that want of accuracy in execution, of which examples fo frequently occur in ancient ftructures. At ten feet from the eaftern window is the eaftern angle of the bujlding. At fourteen feet from the weftern window is a narrow window, three feet wide and about fix feet high, with a femicircular head; and three feet beyond it, is the weftern angle of the building.

Both the eastern and western angles of the wall are regularly chamfered off in the same manner with the angles of the windows. This is, as far as I can recollect, quite singular.

The masonry of every part of the front now remaining, is of peculiar neatness, and the stones are cut to a size nearly-similar to each other, and very small. They are laid in regular and unbroken courses. This sort of accuracy is almost peculiar to the Saxon and early Norman architecture.

The front wall is two feet nine inches in thickness. At sixteen feet eight inches within it is a wall, which, though much ruined, appears to be the original one. There is not the least trace of any partition wall, and the whole space within was probably one large hall or gallery of about one hundred and five feet long, by sixteen feet eight inches wide. The eastern gable is completely demolished, and replaced by houses. In the western gable is a double-headed window, much defaced, but of a design similar to those already described, though rather smaller: its bottom was nearly level with the top of the front wall. It is not easy to decide whether there originally was a floor in the building; but, from the circum-

ftance of the central windows defcending two
feet lower than the lateral ones, I am inclined
to think that there was, and that thefe windows opened quite down to it, forming a fort
of open portico towards the fea. For whatever purpofe this edifice was defigned, its.
whole ftyle and difpofition differ fo materially
from any other with which I am acquainted,
that I cannot but confider it as an object of
confiderable curiofity. If, as I fuppofe, it was
a dwelling or palace, it is among the few remains yet exifting of the habitations of our anceftors, diftinct from monaftic or caftellated
manfions. Perhaps I indulge but a fond
conjecture, when I confider it as poffibly the
hall from which Canute, furrounded by his
courtiers, viewed the rifing tide; and from
whence he defcended to the beach, according
to that moft interefting narrative of our old
hiftorians, to reprefs, by a ftriking and impref-

ACCOUNT

OF

ANTIQUITIES

DISCOVERED AT THE

ANCIENT ROMAN STATION,

CLAUSENTUM (now BITTERN),

Near Southampton;

In a Letter to the Conductor of the Hampshire Repository:

WITH

ADDITIONAL PARTICULARS,

RELATING TO SOME RECENT DISCOVERIES.

By Sir H. C. ENGLEFIELD, Bart.

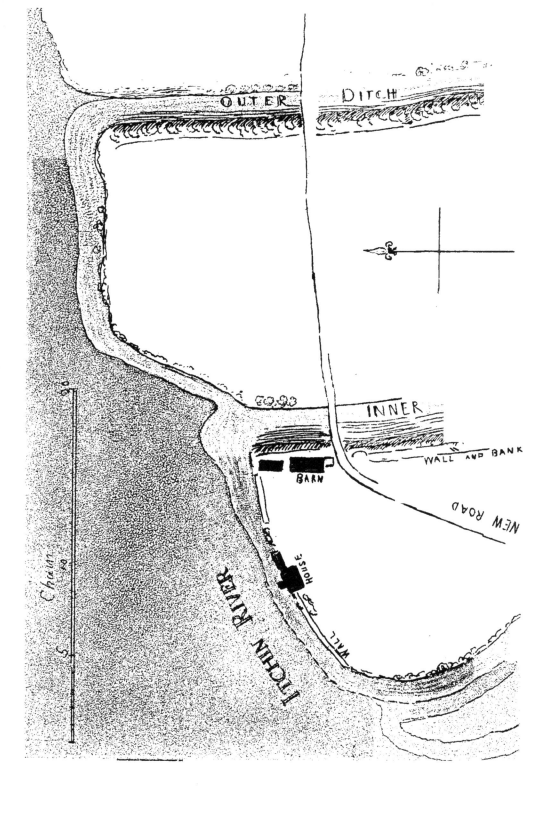

ACCOUNT

OF

ANTIQUITIES

DISCOVERED

At CLAUSENTUM, &c.

To the Conductor of the Hampshire Repository.

Southampton, Jan. 1800.

DEAR SIR,

IN compliance with your wifh I fend you the drawings I have made of the antiquities now exifting at Bittern, and fuch few obfervations on them as I have been able to make.

It does not appear to me that any ftones have been difcovered that ever formed part of a column or femi-column. Thofe which have been taken for femi-columns, one of which is given in the plate, fig. 5, are evidently parts of the coping of fome large edifice; for their curve is reverfed, and dies away againft the fhoulder like a cima. But fig. 6 puts the matter beyond a doubt; for this is the corner ſtone of the ſame coping; and the convex part goes off two ways at a right angle; and the ſquare die at their union has probably had ſome ornament affixed to it, as cramp-holes appear in it. The coping ſtones are of different lengths, from three to four feet, and are twelve in number, including ſome which ſtill remain in the foundation of a ſmall turret or baſtion projecting outwards from the line of the eaſtern Roman wall, and from which foundation thoſe lying looſe at preſent have been lately dug. Near theſe, in the foundation of a part of the ſame turret, remains a ſmall fragment of a very mutilated cornice, fig. 4, which probably belonged to the finall edifice next mentioned.

With theſe ſtones lies the one figured 1, 2, and 3. This formed half the front of ſome ſmall projecting building, or niche for the reception of a ſtatue. Fig. 2 ſhows, by the return of the fluted architrave, and ſome part of an ornament on the frieze, that it was a corner ſtone. The curvature of the niche proves that it was half the frontiſpiece. The central part of the frieze is excavated to receive a thin ſlab, probably of marble, with an inſcription. This

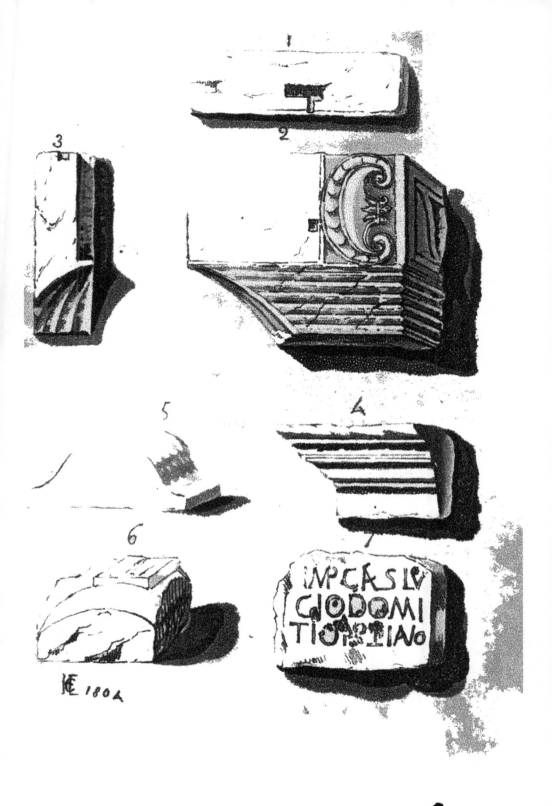

1

2

3

4

5

6

IMPCÆS·LV
CIODOMITI
TIO·N·P·TIANO

ÆE 1804

Inch'd. as the Act directs Jan.ᵉ 1805 by T. Baker & Son Southampt.

was faftened by cramps, the holes of which are vifible in fig. 2 and 3, and from one of which I took a piece of lead which had faftened the iron. The top of the ftone, fig. 1, has, befides the cramp hole in front, a larger towards the back, which fixed it to the wall; and a deeper hole, which either was a lewis hole for raifing it, or ferved to connect it by a pin or tenon with the cornice. Fig 3, the end view of the ftone, fhows the depth of the hollowed part of the frieze where the tablet was placed. The fculpture of this ftone is not very bad: the lunated fhield often occurs on fepulchral ftones. The flutings or grooves in the architrave, which die away againft the niche, are of a fingular and very corrupt tafte. The niche was formed into a fhell; which is an ornament, I believe, only ufed in the later ages. Probably this building, for whatever ufe intended, may be of the age of Aurelian; an infcription to whofe honour I fhall prefently mention.

Fig 7 is as exact a copy as I could make of an infcription which was dug up fome time fince, and is now preferved in the farm houfe at Bittern. The ftone does not appear to have been fquared, or even regularly cut, except on the face on which the infcription is engraved; yet, from its upright form, it does not feem adapted to have been part of a wall. It evidently never was wider than it is, nor pro_bably much higher. The infcription is in letter of tolerably good form, and, except the laft word, which is much effaced, probably by the point of the pickaxe that difcovered it, is perfectly legible. This laft word by accurate infpection may ftill be traced, and the infcription is as follows. IMP CÆS LVCIO DO-MITIO AVRELIANO. In the drawing I have been particularly attentive to mark the fmall remains of the connected letters AVR and EL that it may be feen how far this reading is juftified. There can however be very little doubt refpecting the word, when it is confidered that the only perfon who affumed the purple with the names of Lucius Domitius, was an Egyptian ufurper, of the name of Lucius Domitius Domitian, in the time of Dioclefian, who for two or three years maintained his rebellion at Alexandria. It is utterly improbable that fuch a ufurper fhould have been commemorated in this remote ifland.

On the beach lies a very rude capital, which was worked into the Roman weft wall. The leaves are juft marked out, and the whole is fo very bad, both in defign and execution, that I am much in doubt whether it is not fome Saxon capital ftuck in to mend a breach in the wall, in the period when this ancient ftation was a caftellated manfion.

In the farm houfe is another fmall ftone, which feems to have had four letters cut on it. I only mention it to fay, that it is totally, and, I believe, irrecoverably illegible.

The Roman wall itfelf is fingular in its conftruction. Its height cannot be afcertained. Its thicknefs is about nine feet, and its materials flint, faced very roughly with fquare fmall ftones, and a bending courfe of large flat bricks running through its interior part; but it is extraordinary that it has no foundation whatever, but is literally fet down on the furface of the ground, and is therefore undermined by the waters of the Itchen, which only reach it at fpring tides. A large bank of earth is thrown up againft it on the inner fide; and, in the only place where I have been able to examine its interior conftruction, it feems as if, at a diftance of about nine feet within the outer wall, another wall of about two feet thick has been erected, feemingly as a fort of ftrengthening to the rampart of earth. Of this however I do not fpeak with certainty.

Within the area of the ancient wall, the remains of two very coarfe pavements, or rather plaifter floors, are vifible: one in the bank to the left of the new road, which has been in part wafhed away by the Itchen; the other in the ditch to the right of the road, about midway between the two walls. In digging very lately in the field, a fragment of plaifter was thrown up, painted with a durable red colour, with a narrow white ftripe on it. It feems not unworthy of remark, that the whole foil, as well within the wall as between the wall and outer ditch marked in your *Plan*, is full, not only of fragments of bricks and tiles of various forms, but of fmall pieces of that beautiful earthen ware, the colour, polifh, and grain of which when broken, refemble fine fealing wax more than any fubftance I know of. The ditches dug through thefe fields for the new road have afforded me near a hundred pieces of this ware; fome of them plain, fome embofſed with animals, mafks, thyrfi, lyres, ears of corn, and poppies. As this ware is not uncommonly found in Roman ftations in this country, and more perfect fpecimens than any of mine have been engraved, I have not fent you any drawings of them. The fubjects appear to be nearly fimilar in all that have been found, and are evidently of a myftic tendency. An ornament at the top of the emboffed part, like a deep feftooned fringe with taffels between each feftoon, is almoft univerfal in them. Thofe fragments that are plain appear to be of forms not much adapted to the ufes of common life, being moftly difhes from 6 to 10 inches diameter, with a low upright rim, and ftanding on a fmall foot, not unlike old-fafhioned filver falvers. It has been therefore imagined that thefe were all of them facred utenfils, and probably imported into this country for the purpofe of facrifice. One of the fragments in my poffeffion has been perforated with very neat radiated holes, in regular order, fo as to ferve as a cullender. Thefe holes have been drilled after the veffel was baked. A few fragments have occurred of a fine black ware, nearly as thin as Wedgwood's ware, and covered with a metallic luftre; this is perhaps owing to long lying under ground. Fragments of vafes, of a coarfe earth, not finer than our garden pots, are pretty common; and fome of thefe appear to have been of very confiderable fize. The

P

largeſt were red, ſome others of a dirty brown, like unbaked clay. Thoſe in which aſhes and coins have been found were of the latter ſort. One of theſe, the fragments of which are now

tor of Bittern, preſented, when found, a moſt ſingular appearance. The veſſel containing the bones and aſhes, was encloſed within another which nearly fitted it, and whoſe mouth was ſo narrow as by no means to have admitted it in its hardened ſtate: of this Mr. Waring aſſured me from his own inſpection. The fragments which I ſaw are now ſo mutilated, as not to allow means of aſcertaining the fact by meaſurement of the diameters of the veſſels or their mouths; but both of them bear marks of the potter's lathe, both within and without, and therefore muſt have been ſeparately made. Probably the outer veſſel muſt have been originally broken, and then its parts placed round the inner one when buried, by way of ſecurity from injury.

Several ivory or bone pins were found in the ſame field, ſuch as Sir Chriſtopher Wren mentions having diſcovered in digging the foundation of St. Paul's. Theſe are from three to four inches in length, with blunt points and round heads, and were probably used for faftening the fhrouds in which bodies were buried.

A fine and perfect glafs urn was alfo found, but it has been unfortunately deftroyed.

I cannot clofe this fubject without taking fome notice of the more modern remains extant on this curious fpot, particularly as they probably will not exift much longer in their prefent ftate. The farm houfe, though very old, is built in the ruined walls of a ftately Saxon or Norman edifice. Some columns half buried, but of very neat work, and parts of two ornamented round-headed windows, fubfift at the weft end of the houfe; and in the weft front of the barn are four windows,* of peculiarly excellent mafonry, and very uncommon form. The part of the gateway, yet fubfifting, is probably of the fame date, and equally good work.

Few fpots can be found more interefting, either to an antiquary or a painter, than Bittern in its prefent ftate. From the Roman wall we fee the Saxon remains mingled with

---

* This barn has lately been taken down.

thofe of the 15th century. On the oppofite
fhore is the old brick manfion of Northam,
with its elegant fluted chimnies.   A little fur-

fius's ruined chapel attracts the eye; while the
fpires and towers of the venerable Southampton, full of curious and undefcribed* remains
of antiquity, of almoft every date, from the
earlieft Saxon to the age of James the Firft,
form a diftance to the weft.

. The fweeps of the Itchen, with their bold
fhores covered with hanging woods of noble
oaks, prefent on every fide fcenes of unrivalled
beauty; and the name of Bevis Mount unites
the recollection of an old, and perhaps fabu-
lous, Britifh hero, with that of a man whofe
courage and adventures were fcarcely lefs ro-
mantic than thofe of the moft famous Paladins,
and who, to thefe high qualities, added a re-
fined tafte for elegant art and polite literature.
What Englifhman can look without refpect on
the fhades where the Earl of Peterborough
walked with Arbuthnot and Pope ! Your
Hampfhire readers will, I truft, forgive me, if,

---

* This was written before the publication of the
" Walk through Southampton."

I add, with peculiar and perfonal intereft, that this claffical fpot has not long fince been haunted by another poet.

I hope, Sir, you will excufe a digreffion from the principal object of this letter, which has been fuggefted by the fenfations I have experienced in the many vifits I have paid to this interefting fpot; and believe me

Yours, &c.

H. C. ENGLEFIELD.

ADDITIONAL DISCOVERIES

MADE AT BITTERN,

In 1804 and 1805.

———

DURING the courfe of the laft fummer, confiderable difcoveries have been made at Bittern, by the prefent proprietor, Henry Simpfon, efq; who has with laudable care preferved every fragment of antiquity brought to light in the courfe of the excavations made by him for various purpofes of improvement: and to the politenefs of that gentleman, and the obfervations made on the fpot by my friend Dr. Latham, of Romfey, I am indebted for the information now added to my former account of Bittern.

The whole of the ground was full of fragments of the fame fine red pottery already defcribed, but nothing particularly worthy of notice among them occurred, excepting one fragment of a large fhallow veffel, which had a perforation in its fide, ornamented externally with a lion's head, of coarfe work, which feems to have ferved for a fpout. On the bottom of many of the fragments were impreffed names, probably of the makers; of thefe Dr. Latham fent me the following: CRESCENI; SEVE-RI; MALIVRN; AMATICICI; SACRI·OF; LVPIM; AESFIVINA; CVFF; ACOM; LVPPA; CEN...; MACIOF; DOECA; EPPN; OF·SAB; ADIECTIM; OF·NIGRI. And on the fide of one large fragment, repre-fenting a ftag hunt, is the word ADVOCISI, in a larger and fairer letter than the other ftamps.

Several coins were found, moftly of the lower empire, but none which appear to be cu-rious or rare.

On the north fide of the new road, and nearly half way between the wall and the bridge, a very confiderable number of fke-letons was found, not lefs than fifty. They were laid eaft and weft, and had apparently been buried in coffins of wood faftened with iron nails, of which a great many were found with fmall portions of wood adhering to them.

It is remarkable that all the teeth in every one
of the Jaws were quite perfect, a circumſtance
which ſeems to indicate that the bodies were of
young men, probably of ſoldiers, ſlain in ſome
engagement; evidently, however, by the mode
of ſepulture, at a period later than the Roman
inhabitancy of the ſpot.

Juſt within the outer foſſe, and a little ſouth
of the road, a hollow has been found, which
ſeems to have been either a well or a ſmall
winding ſtaircaſe. Within the inner foſſe another well has been diſcovered, about two feet
and a half in diameter. When found, it was
empty to about eight feet deep; in it was a
human ſkeleton, under the neck of which was
a large ſtone with a hole in it. This circumſtance renders it probable, that the perſon,
whoſe remains were thus found, had been
murdered by drowning in the well, with a
ſtone faſtened to the neck.

The well has ſince been cleared out to the
depth of ten or twelve feet; and in it were
found two ancient iron keys, much corroded;
and a perfect metal jug, holding three pints,
and nearly of the form of an old-faſhioned
ewer. Its form does not induce me to ſuppoſe it Roman.

'The moſt material diſcoveries, however, were made by Mr. Simpſon in the courſe of levelling and filling the inner foſſe, north of the road, for the purpoſe of making a kitchen garden. The whole of the ancient eaſtern wall has by this means been traced. It terminated to the north in a round tower of ſolid maſonry. This tower was about eighteen feet in diameter; and Mr. Simpſon has diſcovered traces of a ſimilar tower at the ſouthern extremity of the wall. Theſe two towers were probably Roman, and parts of the original wall; but at the diſtance of about ſeventy-eight feet from the northern tower, another ſemicircular tower or buttreſs was diſcovered, of twenty-four feet in diameter; whoſe foundations were compoſed of very large ſtones, taken from ſome more ancient building. Several of theſe were ſimilar to thoſe which were deſcribed in my former paper, and which I have ſuppoſed to be coping ſtones. Several fragments of different cornices were alſo found; one of them with the mouldings enriched in no contemptible taſte.

A rude baſe of a column was alſo diſcovered, and many ſtones with inſcriptions, ſome nearly illegible, others very fair. Of

thefe the moſt worthy of notice is a very perfect ſmall altar, dedicated to the goddeſs An-
caſta; a deity hitherto unknown to antiquaries, and therefore of confiderable curiofity.
It is likely that ſhe was ſome local divinity or
tutelary nymph, but the name does not lead
to a probable ſurmife to what country ſhe belonged. It would be too bold a conjecture to
ſuppoſe, from the firſt ſyllable, that ſhe was
connected with the river An' or Ant, of which
we have ſpoken in the beginning of this work:
but it may not, poſſibly, be foreign from the
ſubject to obſerve, that the Gauliſh and Britiſh
goddeſs of victory was called Andate or An-
draſte.

The annexed repreſentation is I believe very
accurate: it is to a ſcale of an inch to a foot,
as are thoſe of the other inſcriptions. The
inſcriptions themſelves are copied with great
care, after impreſſions taken from the ſtones
themſelves.

The infcription may bé thus read : DEÆ
ANCASTÆ GEMINVS MANIVS LIBENS
MERITO; for if the letters VSLM, in the
laft line, be fuppofed to ftand for " votum fol-
vit libens merito," as they often do, the proper
name muft be Mani, which is of an unufual
form.

tended to be fixed againſt a wall.

I dare not hazard any reading of the inſcription, which is of very rude workmanſhip.

The three following are votive or dedicatory. The firſt is to the emperor Gordian, probably the younger.

It is of very rude work, and may be read as follows: IMPERATORI CÆSARI MARCO ANTONIO GORDIANO PIO FELICI AVGVSTO.RP.B.I. Of the three Gordians, the youngeſt only bore the name of Pius; but it is poſſible that the letter P might not be the name of the emperor, but one of the uſual titles, Pius, Felix.

The next is to the emperors Gallius and Volufianus.

It is as rude as poffible, but eafily legible: IMPERATORIBVS CÆSARIBVS GALLO ET VOLVSIANO AVGVSTIS.

The laſt is to the tyrant Tetricus : it is on a ſquare ſtone, and of very neat workmanſhip.

It is not entirely legible, the firſt line being much injured. It may ſafely be read as follows: AP . CA - - CAIO . ÆSVLO . TETRI- CO . PIO . ET . AVGVSTO.

This inſcription is ſingular, from the name of Æſulus preceding that of Tetricus, whoſe family name was Piveſus, or Peſuvius, or Pive- ſuvius ; but neither the father or ſon ever ap- pear to have borne a name approaching to Æſulus ; and though, from the great variety in the ſpelling of the name on different me- dals, its orthography appears to have been un- certain, yet Æſulus is too far diſtant from all the readings, to render it probable that it was intended for any of them.

On the inscriptions found at Bittern we may remark, that four of them are votive to the several emperors named in them. In Horsley's Britannia Romana a few occur in the same form, generally on stones approaching more or less to a columnar shape. Horsley calls them Miliary; which they evidently cannot be, as neither place nor distance is mentioned on them. Besides, the discovery of four on one spot would alone destroy this supposition. From the rudeness of their form, they cannot be supposed to have been the bases of statues; and indeed they seem too rude to have been placed within any temple or public building. Perhaps they might have been mere memorials of the accession of the sovereign whose name they bear, and placed in the Forum or Campus Martius of the station, when its garrison took the oath of allegiance. This, however, must be merely matter of conjecture.

H. C. ENGLEFIELD.

Tilney Street, London,
August 7, 1805.

ADDENDA.

NOTES, &c.

PAGE 35.

The precentorſhip was certainly attached to St. Mary's: for, in the Liber Regis, the living is deſcribed as the " Precentorſhip in the Church of St. Mary near Southampton, alias the Rectory of St. Mary's near Southampton ;" and as the patron of the vicarage of South Stoneham, though incumbent of the former, is again called " *the Precentor* or Rector of St. Mary's near Southampton," might not the Valor of Pope Nicholas IV. probably afford ſome further information, as to what this precentorſhip was; or how it became connected, not with the *right of patronage*, which is not uncommon in the caſe of cathedral precentorſhips, but with the *actual incumbency* of a pariſh church, of which I do not at preſent know of another inſtance ?

PAGE 39.

Arthur Hammond, efq, has lately difcovered, in the records of the Corporation, a deed, with the feal appendent, dated in 1565. In this earlier impreffion of the feal, the infcription round the reverfe is ftill legible, and it runs thus: O . MATER . VIRGO . DEI . TV . MISERERE . NOBIS.

PAGE 70.

In the north fide of Simnel ftreet, and fronting the lane which forms a communication between that ftreet and St. Michael's fquare, is an ancient and curious vaulted apartment, which has long been ufed as a cellar. It is approached, on the fouth, by a defcent of thirteen ftone fteps; on the feventh of which the ancient door was placed, the hooks of its hinges ftill remaining: the prefent door, which is modern, being at the top of the fteps, and level with the ftrect. On entering the apartment; thofe who have feen the ancient room at Netley Abbey, which is called the abbot's kitchen, are ftruck with the refemblance which the two places bear to each other.

The length of this room is thirty-four feet ten inches; the breadth, twenty-one feet feven inches; the extreme height of the vaulting, thirteen feet three inches. In the four corners, and midway between them, on the north and fouth fides, and at the diftance from the corners of fifteen feet each way, at two feet four inches above the floor, the ribs or ramifications of the pointed arches which fupport the ceiling, rife from their refpective groins; which are fupported by heads apparently in their original ftate rudely cut, and at prefent much defaced. The heads are not uniform, and one appears to have fhoulders fupporting it. On thefe heads are femi-octagonal and very deep mouldings; from which rife, in each corner one ramification, and at each fide three ramifications: thefe interfect in two places on the ceiling, and in the centre of the ceiling another ramification is thrown acrofs. At the interfection neareft the eaft end is the ornament of a head with flowing hair and a beard, of tolerable execution. At the other interfection is a carved flower, and the fame at the middle ramification.

The fouth fide of the building, which forms its front in Simnel ftreet, is occupied by the door and windows. The door is in the lower or weftern compartment, and is placed in the middle of one of the arches; the two windows fill up the other. The door way, as was before obferved, is on the feventh ftep below the prefent level of the ftrect. It confifts of a rather obtufe-headed arch, five feet five inches and a half wide, and five feet ten inches high; the fides of the door way going up ftraight to the height of four feet four inches, from which height the arch begins to rife.

In the upper or eaftern compartment of the fouth fide, are two pointed-arched windows, now bricked up. The bottom of thefe is only three feet from the floor; extreme height five feet fix inches; width inwards five feet fix inches, but narrowing towards the ftreet, where the width is only four feet. Width of pier between windows, one foot. In the prefent ftate of this building, the windows are completely buried, their tops being juft about the level of the ftrect.

In the centre of the eaft end is an ancient fire place, projecting into the room like that at Netley, with a kind of flope like a pent houfe, terminating with a large and plain moulding, which is fupported by plain pillars. The front of the fire place is now confiderably damaged, but is faid to have been, within memory, rather handfome; the fide pillars having been ornamented with heads below the moulding, and the middle forming an arch. Beyond the pillars, on each fide, are brackets carefully finifhed with neat and deep mouldings, and terminating at the bottom with a fort of foliage. The chimney place is five feet eight inches wide, projects into the room two feet ten inches, height from the ground of the moulding below the pent houfe five feet two inches, flope of pent houfe three feet two inches, funnel of chimney three feet by fifteen inches. In the north-eaft corner of the room is a ftone-ftair cafe, now bricked up, but which fcarcely feems to have been part of the original plan. And on the weft fide of the room is a door way into an adjoining cellar, alfo bricked up, but evidently, in its original ftate, a modern perforation, and not connected with the building as it was firft erected.

Adjoining this building are fome old cellars; but a careful infpection of them has afforded no light as to their former probable connexion with this place. The only thing remarkable in them is an aperture fomewhat like the buttery hatch in ancient buildings, but which is fo obftructed with brick work that it feems impoffible to determine whether originally it ferved this purpofe, or was merely a cupboard; and at any rate it feems unlikely ever to have had any thing to do with this building, as, if ever it led any where, it muft have been to a place below this.

———————

The following notes were communicated juft as the impreffion of the work was finifhed, by the kindnefs of A. Hammond, efq; to whom the author of this work is already fo much indebted. They could not therefore appear in their proper places.

Page 6.

The building in Houndwell has been taken down while the work was printing.

This building was originally a public wafh-houfe, and was furnifhed with troughs, &c, for that purpofe. In 1634, as appears by 'the town records, it was ordered to be repaired. It not having been ufed for many years, agreeably to its defign, it was lately judged expedient to take it down.

PAGE 8.

In ancient times, the corporation received a toll, for goods, wares, and merchandifes, paf-fing on the bridge at Bargate: and, by an entry in their journal, of 1679, it appears that it was given up, in confideration of a fum of money, raifed by the inhabitants of this and the neighbouring towns.

PAGE 9.

The third coat of arms over Bargate is of Frederick Tylney, efq, who reprefented South-ampton in parliament, in 1702.

The fourth of Thomas Lewis, efq, who re-prefented it in 1715. He was a confiderable benefactor to the town.

It feems, probable that thefe fhields have at times had a change of arms, in compliment of particular benefactors.

There are no means of afcertaining when they were firft put up ; but, in 1702, there is an order " that the king's arms, fcutcheons, gyants, and the dial, at Bargate, be repaired." At that time, we may prefume, fome other arms gave way to thofe of Tylney, he having then prefented to the corporation a grand filver tankard, wafhed with gold.

The fhield occupied by the arms of Wyndham was probably painted in compliment to Sir Charles Wyndham, elected a member for this town in 1679.

Two, of his name, appear to have been recorders of this town ; one chofen in 1690, the other (his brother) in 1696.

PAGE 33.

Holy Rood Church, about 1321, ftood in the middle of the High-ftreet ; and, on its removal, the old audit houfe probably was built on the fame fite. Long fubfequent to this, it was greatly defaced by the erection of butchers' fhambles around it, which theretofore

were near the friary, now Gloucefter-fquare:
and the wardens of the butchers were, in
1634, directed to confine to, either the friars'
gate, or New-corner, now called Butcher-row.

PAGE 46.

Among the attendants or fervants of the
corporation, formerly, was a band of five muficians, who wore gowns and badges; and, on
the eleventh of December, 1607, it was ordered, that the muficians fhould give fecurity
for their efcutcheons or badges of filver.

PAGE 71.

In 1214, Adam De Port was governor of
Southampton caftle. . The family of De Port
appears, from Domefday Book, to have been
of great diftinction, and to have poffeffed
large eftates in thefe parts, foon after the
Conqueft.

PAGE 75.

The fair ufually called Chapel Fair appears,
from the proclamation ufually read on opening

it, to have been granted by Henry VII. In 1628 and 1637 it was forbidden to be held, on account of the plague.

Engraved Title.

The engraved title page, compofed from fragments extant in the town.

·The arch is that mentioned in page 12, as exifting in the room in the town hall, adjoining the grand-jury room.

The bas relief of two heads is noticed in page 32.

The niche work on the ftone, on which the upper part of the title is engraved, is copied from that of the conduit in the High-ftreet, near the friary. See page 47. `

The three monograms at the bottom of the plate are mentioned in page 64. The middle one is that in St. Michael's church; that to the left ·is in St. Mary's church-yard; that to the right, at Romfey.

The Gothic letter in which the title is engraved, is copied from that of the mayoralty feal.

PAGE 21.

Meafured elevation of the five fouthernmoft arches in the town wall, with the more ancient buildings covered by them. This elevation is drawn to a fcale of ten feet to an inch.

PAGE 23.

Another part of the arches in the wall of the town, fhowing the remain of the very fin-gular building, partly deftroyed, and then brought to make a part of the wall. The view comprehends the arches defcribed as eight, nine, ten, and eleven. This elevation is drawn to the fame fcale with the other, being ten feet to an inch.

PAGE 38.

The regalia of the corporation.. The mace, oar, and fword, are not drawn in their real proportions, but are each copied exactly from the originals. The mace is the moft ancient one belonging to the corporation. On each fide are feals. The fhip is copied as exactly as the fize would allow, from the filver mayoralty feal. The three figures in niches are the reverfe of the corporation feal now in ufe. The fhield in the centre has the arms of the town.

PAGE 42.

The two feals defcribed in the note. The large one is the feal for recognizances. The fmall one the feal of the ftaple.

PAGE 50.

View looking weft, in Porters'-lane. The ancient building is on the right. The two remaining céntral windows are feen, and the two lateral windows beyond them on the weſt fide. Between the great opening and the upper window, near the eye, a fmall part of the moulding of the neareſt lateral window to the eaſt of the centre is vifible. The furtheſt eaſtern window is out of the picture. To the left are the warehoufes with the covered footway running under them.

PAGE 63.

Infide view of St. Michael's church, taken from the fouth door, looking north. The gates feen laterally to the right, open into the chancel. The femicircular arches fupport the tower.

PAGE 65.

Font in St. Michael's church. In the compartment to the right of the plate is a fourth part of the top of the font, fhowing its ornaments; and below, an elevation of the font.

View up Blue-anchor-lane, fhowing the fide of the very ancient building mentioned in pages 23.and 68.

Elevation of the central part of the building in Porter's-lane; comprehending the triple great window, and one of the two fmaller windows on each fide of it. The veftiges of the two doors alfo appear. This elevation extends forty-eight feet, and is drawn to a fcale of a quarter of an inch to a foot.

Plan of the Roman ftation at Bittern. The buildings marked *houfe* and *barn* are of high

T

antiquity. Between the barn and new road
was a gateway, now deftroyed. On the other
fide of the road the foundation of the tower is
marked, out of which the large coping ftones
were taken.

The lighter fhading fhows the ground
covered by fpring tides, the darker by ordinary tides. At low water the whole is a
mud bank.

This plan is in great part taken from that
publifhed in the firft volume of the Hampfhire
Repofitory.

PAGE 108.

Antiquities found at Bittern. No. 1, 2,
and 3, are top, fide, and front views of the
ftone fuppofed to have been part of the front
of an ornamented niche. No. 4 is a mutilated cornice. No. 5, one of the coping
ftones erroneoufly called femicolumns. No. 6,
view of a fragment of an angular ftone of the
fame coping. No. 7, an infcription to Aure-

Lightning Source UK Ltd.
Milton Keynes UK
UKHW020635230119
336058UK00012B/637/P